LATIN 101

Mastering the Basics of Latin

MICHAEL SZYMCZYK

Copyright © 2024 Michael Szymczyk

All rights reserved. No part of this book may be used, reproduced, or transmitted in any form without prior permission from the author, except for citations and quotations with attribution. For other uses, please request permission at info@vidart.org.

Szymczyk, Michael, 1981-
Latin 101: Mastering the Basics of Latin
PAPERBACK ISBN: 9798338222379

CONTENTS

PREFACE
Intro with precursory remarks, a pronunciation guide, and the top 200 words to start learning.

CHAPTER 1: Introduction to Latin
1.1 Introduction to Latin

1.2 Personal Pronouns

1.3 Verbs and Conjugations

1.4 Numbers and Time

1.5 Conjugation Patterns (including active and passive voices)

1.6 Vocabulary Building

1.7 The Absence of Articles (Latin does not use definite or indefinite articles)

1.8 Adjectives (including agreement with nouns in gender, number, and case)

1.9 Prepositions (with their corresponding cases)

1.10 Adverbs

1.11 Interjections

1.12 More Vocabulary

1.13 Noun Declensions (covers the five declensions in Latin)

CHAPTER 2: Common Phrases

CHAPTER 3: Grammar
3.1 Moods (Indicative, Imperative, Subjunctive)

3.2 Tenses (including all six Latin tenses: Present, Imperfect, Future, Perfect, Pluperfect, and Future Perfect)

3.3 Negation (use of "non" and other negating words)

3.4 Cases (Nominative, Genitive, Dative, Accusative, Ablative, and Vocative)

3.5 Perfect Tense (Latin does not have a simple past; it uses perfect and imperfect tenses instead)

3.6 Infinitive Constructions (including indirect statements)

3.7 Reflexive Verbs

3.8 Transitive and Intransitive Verbs in Latin

3.9 Passive Voice, Participles, Gerunds & More

CHAPTER 4: Reading Practice

PREFACE

The purpose of this book is to make learning Latin more approachable and effective. I created this as a favor for someone who enjoyed my more comprehensive language learning manual, *German 101*. My goal was to use a similar format to provide an improved learning resource for other languages. While Latin is no longer a spoken language, it remains vital for understanding classical literature, historical texts, and the roots of many modern languages. Unlike living languages, Latin learning focuses more on reading, translating, and understanding its structure and influence, rather than on conversational fluency.

This book is designed not just to teach you the basics of Latin vocabulary, grammar, and syntax, but to guide you in a methodical way that emphasizes mastery of key concepts. Many traditional textbooks may overwhelm you with dry lists of words and rules, expecting you to memorize them without understanding their context or significance. My aim here is a little different: I want to help you grasp the logic of the Latin language, which will make your learning process more intuitive and rewarding.

When I first started learning Latin, I found that much of what I encountered in textbooks was academic and disconnected from the rich cultural and historical contexts that give the language its depth. This book aims to bridge that gap by not only teaching you Latin grammar and vocabulary but also by introducing you to the ways Latin has shaped Western thought, literature, and more.

The first two chapters of this book will introduce you to the foundational vocabulary and phrases you need to know. While this may seem like a straightforward task, it's important to approach it with the goal of building a strong foundation that will support your understanding of more complex texts. These chapters will cover the essential words and phrases you need, alongside clear explanations of their usage.

The subsequent chapters will delve deeper into the grammatical structures that are crucial for reading and translating Latin texts. We'll explore verb conjugations, noun declensions, and the various cases used in Latin, helping you to understand how the language functions on a deeper level.

Given that Latin is a highly structured language, mastering these grammatical rules is essential for accurate translation and comprehension. However, learning Latin also involves immersing yourself in the language as it was used by the Romans. Although you won't be conversing in Latin, immersing yourself in classical texts, inscriptions, and even modern adaptations of Latin will deepen your understanding and retention of the language.

This book does not include extensive quizzes, as Latin learning is often better reinforced through practice and repetition of translation exercises rather than rote memorization. Instead, I encourage you to engage with Latin through reading and translation exercises.

While Latin may seem daunting at first, with its complex system of cases, tenses, and moods, I believe that with the right approach, it can be both manageable and intellectually rewarding. By the end of this book, you will have a solid foundation in Latin and be well-prepared to explore its literature, philosophy, and historical documents.

Pronunciation Guide

Vowels

- **A**: Pronounced like *ah* in "father," but shorter for short *a*.
  Example: *pater* (pah-ter, meaning "father").
- **E**: Pronounced like *eh* in "met" for short *e*, and like *ey* in "they" for long *ē*.
  Example: *mēns* (mains, meaning "mind").
- **I**: Pronounced like *ee* in "see" for long *ī* and *i* in "sit" for short *i*.
  Example: *vīnum* (wee-num, meaning "wine").
- **O**: Pronounced like *oh* in "so" for long *ō*, and like *o* in "off" for short *o*.
  Example: *domus* (doh-moos, meaning "house").
- **U**: Pronounced like *oo* in "food" for long *ū*, and like *u* in "put" for short *u*.
  Example: *lūna* (loo-nah, meaning "moon").

Consonants

- **B**: Pronounced like *b* in "bed."
  Example: *bellum* (bel-lum, meaning "war").
- **C**: Always pronounced like *k* in "cat," regardless of the following vowel.
  Example: *casa* (kah-sah, meaning "cottage" or "hut").
- **D**: Pronounced like *d* in "dog."
  Example: *dominus* (doh-mee-noos, meaning "master" or "lord").
- **F**: Pronounced like *f* in "fish."
  Example: *filius* (fee-lee-oos, meaning "son").
- **G**: Always pronounced like *g* in "go," regardless of the following vowel.
  Example: *gladius* (glah-dee-oos, meaning "sword").
- **H**: Pronounced as a light aspirate, like *h* in "house."
  Example: *honor* (hoh-nor, meaning "honor").
- **I** (as a consonant): Pronounced like *y* in "yes."
  Example: *Iulius* (yoo-lee-oos, meaning "Julius").
- **K**: Rare, but pronounced like *k* in "kite."
  Example: *kalendae* (kah-len-dae, meaning "calends," the first day of the month).
- **L**: Pronounced like *l* in "love."
  Example: *līber* (lee-ber, meaning "free").
- **M**: Pronounced like *m* in "man."
  Example: *māter* (mah-ter, meaning "mother").

- **N**: Pronounced like *n* in "no."
  Example: *nox* (noks, meaning "night").
- **P**: Pronounced like *p* in "pan."
  Example: *pater* (pah-ter, meaning "father").
- **Q**: Always followed by *u* and pronounced like *kw* in "quick."
  Example: *quī* (kwee, meaning "who").
- **R**: Slightly rolled, similar to the *r* in Scottish English.
  Example: *rex* (reks, meaning "king").
- **S**: Always pronounced like *s* in "see," never as *z* in "rise."
  Example: *serpens* (ser-pens, meaning "snake").
- **T**: Pronounced like *t* in "tap," without the *sh* sound as in "nation."
  Example: *templum* (tem-ploom, meaning "temple").
- **V**: Pronounced like *w* in "wine."
  Example: *via* (wee-ah, meaning "road" or "way").
- **X**: Pronounced like *ks* in "kicks."
  Example: *dux* (duks, meaning "leader" or "general").
- **Z**: Pronounced like *dz* in "adze."
  Example: *zēphyrus* (dzay-fi-roos, meaning "west wind").

Syllable Stress: Latin words typically stress the penultimate syllable if it is long; otherwise, the antepenultimate syllable is stressed.

Diphthongs: Latin diphthongs include:

- *ae* pronounced like "ai" in "aisle" (e.g., *caelum* - "sky").
- *au* pronounced like "ow" in "how" (e.g., *autumnus* - "autumn").
- *oe* pronounced like "oi" in "boil" (e.g., *poena* - "penalty").

Special Consonant Combinations

- **CH** pronounced like 'k': *chorus* (koh-roos, meaning "chorus" or "dance")
- **PH** pronounced like 'p' as in "philosophy": *philosophia* (pee-loh-soh-fee-ah, meaning "philosophy")
- **TH** pronounced like 't': *theātrum* (tay-ah-troom, meaning "theater")
- **GN** like 'ny' in "canyon": *gnōscere* (nyoh-skeh-reh, meaning "to know")

Key Grammatical Terms in Latin with Examples

Noun (Nomen) - Identifies people, places, or things.
Latin: *Canis* (meaning "dog")

Pronoun (Pronomen) - Replaces a noun.
Latin: *Ille est laetus.* (meaning "He is happy.")

Adjective (Adiectivum) - Describes a noun.
Latin: *Flos pulcher* (meaning "A beautiful flower")

Verb (Verbum) - Indicates an action, state, or occurrence.
Latin: *Currit.* (meaning "He/She/It runs.")

Adverb (Adverbium) - Modifies verbs, adjectives, or other adverbs.
Latin: *Celeriter currit.* (meaning "He/She/It runs quickly.")

Preposition (Praepositio) - Shows the relationship between a noun or pronoun and other words in a sentence.
Latin: *Liber super mensa* (meaning "The book on the table")

Conjunction (Coniunctio) - Connects words, phrases, or clauses.
Latin: *Cantat et saltat.* (meaning "He/She sings and dances.")

Interjection (Interiectio) - Expresses emotion.
Latin: *Heu! Quam terribile!* (meaning "Alas! How terrible!")

Participle (Participium) - A verb form used as an adjective.
Latin: *Aqua currens* (meaning "Running water")

Infinitive (Infinitivus) - The basic form of a verb.
Latin: *Currere* (meaning "to run")

Gerund (Gerundium) - A verb form that functions as a noun.
Latin: *Currere est iucundum.* (meaning "Running is pleasant.")

Passive Voice (Vox Passiva) - The subject is the recipient of the action.
Latin: *Panis editur ab eo.* (meaning "The bread is eaten by him.")

Active Voice (Vox Activa) - The subject performs the action.
Latin: *Panem edit.* (meaning "He/She eats the bread.")

Predicate (Praedicatum) - The part of a sentence or clause stating something about the subject.
Latin: *Pueri ludunt.* (meaning "The boys play.")

Subject (Subiectum) - The part of a sentence or clause that indicates what it is about.
Latin: *Canis latrat.* (meaning "The dog barks.")

Object (Obiectum) - Receives the action of the verb.
Latin: *Librum legit.* (meaning "He/She reads the book.")

Clause (Clausula) - A group of words with a subject and a predicate.
Latin: *Domum venire vult.* (meaning "He/She wants to come home.")

Phrase (Locutio) - A group of words without a subject-predicate component.
Latin: *In horto* (meaning "in the garden")

Determiner (Determinans) - Modifies a noun to show reference.
Latin: *Hic liber est bonus.* (meaning "This book is good.")

IMPORTANT WORDS TO LEARN AT THE START

- **Ita** (yes) - (ee-tah)
- **Nōn** (no) - (nohn)
- **Fortasse** (maybe) - (for-tahs-seh)
- **Quis** (who) - (kwees)
- **Quid** (what) - (kwid)
- **Quandō** (when) - (kwan-doh)
- **Ubi** (where) - (oo-bee)
- **Cūr** (why) - (koor)
- **Quōmodo** (how) - (kwoh-mo-doh)
- **Et** (and) - (eht)
- **Sum, Esse** (to be) - (soom, eh-seh)
- **In** (in) - (in)
- **Ad** (to) - (ahd)
- **Habeō** (to have) - (hah-beh-oh)
- **Ego** (I) - (eh-go)
- **Fīo** (to become) - (fee-oh)
- **Ea, Eī, Eae** (she, they) - (eh-ah, eh-ee, eh-ae)
- **Dē** (from, of) - (deh)
- **Cum** (with) - (koom)
- **Is** (he, it) - (ees)
- **Sē** (oneself) - (seh)
- **Etiam** (also) - (eh-tee-ahm)
- **Super** (on, above) - (soo-pehr)
- **Pro** (for) - (proh)
- **Quod** (that, because) - (kwod)
- **Ergo** (therefore, thus) - (ehr-goh)
- **Possum** (can, to be able) - (poh-soom)
- **Hic, Haec, Hoc** (this) - (heek, hāyk, hock)
- **Suus, Sua, Suum** (his, her, their) - (soo-oos, soo-ah, soo-oom)
- **Sīc** (thus, so) - (seek)
- **Vel** (or) - (wehl)
- **Nōs** (we) - (nohs)
- **Sed** (but) - (sehd)
- **Tum** (then) - (toom)
- **Ūnus** (one) - (oo-noos)
- **Illic** (there) - (ihl-lik)
- **Annum** (year) - (ah-noom)
- **Tū** (you) - (too)
- **Meus, Mea, Meum** (my) - (meh-oos, meh-ah, meh-oom)
- **Iam** (already) - (yahm)
- **Ante** (before, in front of) - (ahn-teh)
- **Per** (through) - (pehr)

- **Dō** (to give) - (doh)
- **Magis** (more) - (mah-gis)
- **Alius, Alia, Aliud** (other) - (ah-lee-oos, ah-lee-ah, ah-lee-ood)
- **Multus, Multa, Multum** (much, a lot) - (mool-toos, mool-tah, mool-toom)
- **Venio** (to come) - (weh-nee-oh)
- **Nunc** (now) - (noonk)
- **Mihi** (to me, for me) - (mee-hee)
- **Volō** (to want) - (woh-loh)
- **Omnis, Omne** (all) - (ohm-nees, ohm-neh)
- **Semper** (always) - (sehm-pehr)
- **Eō** (to go) - (eh-oh)
- **Valdē** (very) - (wahl-deh)
- **Hīc** (here) - (heek)
- **Etiamsī** (even though) - (eh-tee-ahm-see)
- **Usque** (until) - (oos-kweh)
- **Magnus, Magna, Magnum** (big, large) - (mahg-noos, mahg-nah, mahg-noom)
- **Iterum** (again) - (ee-teh-room)
- **Tempus** (time) - (tehm-poos)
- **Duo** (two) - (doo-oh)
- **Bonus, Bona, Bonum** (good) - (boh-noos, boh-nah, boh-noom)
- **Sciō** (to know [a fact]) - (skee-oh)
- **Videō** (to see) - (wee-deh-oh)
- **Relinquō** (to leave behind) - (reh-leen-kwoh)
- **Nōs** (us) - (nohs)
- **Quia** (because) - (kwee-ah)
- **Sub** (under) - (soob)
- **Multus, Multī** (many) - (mool-toos, mool-tee)
- **Stō** (to stand) - (stoh)
- **Omnis, Omne** (each, every) - (ohm-nees, ohm-neh)
- **Exemplum** (example) - (ehk-sehm-ploohm)
- **Prīmus, Prīma, Prīmum** (first) - (pree-moos, pree-mah, pree-moom)
- **Accipiō** (to receive, get) - (ahk-kee-pee-oh)
- **Vīvō** (to live) - (wee-woh)
- **Cōgitō** (to think) - (koh-gee-toh)
- **Sūmō** (to take) - (soo-moh)
- **Pars** (part) - (pahrs)
- **Labor** (work) - (lah-bohr)
- **Annum** (year) - (ah-noom)
- **Venio** (to come) - (weh-nee-oh)
- **Rogō** (to ask) - (roh-goh)
- **Cognoscō** (to know [a person]) - (koh-nyohs-koh)
- **Dormiō** (to sleep) - (dohr-mee-oh)
- **Cēnō** (to eat) - (keh-noh)
- **Lūdō** (to play) - (loo-doh)
- **Legō** (to read) - (leh-goh)
- **Scrībō** (to write) - (skree-boh)
- **Currō** (to run) - (koor-roh)
- **Natō** (to swim) - (nah-toh)
- **Volō** (to fly) - (woh-loh)
- **Incipiō** (to begin) - (een-kee-pee-oh)
- **Intellegō** (to understand) - (in-tehl-leh-goh)
- **Ponō** (to put, set) - (poh-noh)
- **Ostendō** (to show) - (ohs-tehn-doh)
- **Dūcō** (to lead) - (doo-koh)
- **Exspectō** (to wait for) - (ehk-spehk-toh)
- **Sperō** (to hope) - (speh-roh)
- **Adiuvo** (to help) - (ah-dee-yoo-woh)
- **Inveniō** (to find) - (een-wehn-ee-oh)
- **Amittō** (to lose) - (ah-mit-toh)
- **Quaerō** (to search, look for) - (kwai-roh)
- **Mutō** (to change) - (moo-toh)
- **Significō** (to mean, signify) - (sig-nee-fee-koh)
- **Decernō** (to decide) - (deh-kehr-noh)
- **Narrō** (to tell, narrate) - (nah-roh)
- **Teneō** (to hold) - (teh-neh-oh)

- **Oblivīscor** (to forget) - (oh-blih-wee-skor)
- **Pecūnia** (money) - (peh-koo-nee-ah)

Additional Common Words & Phrases:

- **Domina** (Mrs., Lady) - (doh-mee-nah)
- **Virgō** (Ms., Maiden) - (weer-goh)
- **Dominus** (Mr., Lord) - (doh-mee-noos)
- **Salvē** (Hello, singular) - (sahl-way)
- **Salvēte** (Hello, plural) - (sahl-way-teh)
- **Avē** (Greetings, Hail) - (ah-way)
- **Ignōsce mihi** (Excuse me) - (ig-noh-skeh mee-hee)
- **Quaēsō** (Please) - (kwai-soh)
- **Bene** (Good, Well) - (beh-neh)
- **Valē** (Goodbye, singular) - (wah-lay)
- **Valēte** (Goodbye, plural) - (wah-lay-teh)
- **Grātiās tibi agō** (Thank you) - (grah-tee-ahs tee-bee ah-goh)
- **Nihil est** (You're welcome, It's nothing) - (nee-hil ehst)
- **Ita** (Yes) - (ee-tah)
- **Nōn** (No) - (nohn)
- **Ignōsce mihi** (Sorry) - (ig-noh-skeh mee-hee)
- **Quid agis?** (How are you? to one person) - (kwid ah-gees)
- **Bene sum** (I'm fine) - (beh-neh soom)
- **Nōn intellegō** (I don't understand) - (nohn in-tehl-leh-goh)
- **Lōquerisne Anglicē?** (Do you speak English?) - (loh-kweh-rees-ne ang-lee-keh)
- **Amō tē** (I love you) - (ah-moh tay)

Pronunciation Guide:

Domina (doh-mee-nah): Emphasize "nah" with a resonant and clear pronunciation.
Domina parva (doh-mee-nah par-wah): Flow smoothly through "doh-mee-nah," and finish with a crisp "par-wah."
Dominus (doh-mee-noos): Focus on the nasal "mee" and lightly emphasize "noos."
Audi (ow-dee): A short, vibrant "ow" followed by a clear "dee."
Patruus (pah-troo-oos): Each syllable should be enunciated clearly, with slight emphasis on "roo."
Ignosce mihi (eeg-noh-skeh mee-kee): Ensure clarity in each syllable, with emphasis on "noh-skeh."
Quaeso (kwai-soh): Pronounce each syllable distinctly, flowing smoothly from one to the next.
Salve/Bene mane (sahl-weh/beh-neh mah-neh): Keep "Salve" cheerful and light; "Bene mane" should sound bright and welcoming.
Bona vespera (boh-nah weh-speh-rah): Pronounce "Bona" smoothly, followed by a clear and distinct "vespera."
Vale (wah-leh): Emphasize the "leh" slightly, lingering gently.
Gratias tibi (grah-tee-ahs tee-bee): Stress "tee" part, blending smoothly into "ahs."
Nihil est (nee-hil est): Ensure each syllable is clear and distinct, with slight emphasis on "hil."

Ita (ee-tah): A sharp, clear pronunciation.

Non (nohn): Pronounced firmly and briefly.

Ignosce (eeg-noh-skeh): Emphasize "noh," with a slight pause after "s."

Quomodo vales? (kwoh-moh-doh wah-les): Flow smoothly from "Quomodo" to "vales," with emphasis on "wah."

Bene sum (beh-neh soom): Make sure "Bene" is smooth, with a clear and upbeat "soom."

Non intellego (nohn een-tehl-leh-goh): Pronounce each syllable distinctly, stressing "tehl."

Loquerisne Latine? (loh-kweh-rees-neh lah-tee-neh): Ensure "Loquerisne" flows smoothly, with a clear "lah-tee-neh" to finish.

Amo te (ah-moh teh): Pronounce "Amo" warmly, followed by a soft yet emphatic "teh."

Chapter 1: An Introduction to Latin

The Romans referred to their language as *Latīna* and to their homeland as *Latium* (the region surrounding Rome). *Latīna* is pronounced "lah-tee-nah." The Romans identified themselves as *Rōmānī* (ro-mah-nee) when referring to men or a mixed group, and *Rōmānae* (ro-mah-nai) for women. Epic tales, such as Virgil's *Aeneid*, reflect the Romans' view of themselves as the cultural and mythological descendants of the Trojans. This belief finds some support in historical and genetic evidence suggesting that some of the Etruscans, particularly ruling members of the elite, who significantly influenced Roman culture, may have migrated from the region near ancient Troy.

The Etruscans, known for their advanced civilization in northern Italy, contributed profoundly to Roman life, including religion, architecture, and elements of the Latin language. For instance, Latin words such as *rex* (king), *triumphus* (triumph), *gladius* (sword), and *templum* (temple) have roots in the Etruscan language, reflecting their cultural impact. Moreover, several early Roman kings, such as Tarquinius Priscus and Servius Tullius, were of Etruscan origin, highlighting the deep connection between these civilizations. This cultural blending helped shape the Roman identity and reinforced their belief in being the rightful heirs to the legacy of Troy.

The Romans took immense pride in their cultural heritage, which they believed linked them to the ancient and noble traditions of the East. This belief was not merely mythological but a cornerstone of their worldview, influencing their politics, military ambitions, and sense of destiny. The concept of *Romanitas*—the qualities that defined the Roman way of life—was inseparably tied to their understanding of their origins, both historical and legendary. This connection to Troy and the East also influenced Rome's expansionist policies, as the Romans saw themselves as bearers of civilization, destined to spread their culture and influence across the known world.

Latin, an Italic language, has had a profound and lasting influence as the ancestor of the Romance languages, including Italian, French, Spanish, Portuguese, and Romanian. Many English words also derive from Latin roots, so English speakers may recognize familiar vocabulary. However, caution is necessary, as not all words that look similar share the same meaning in both languages. For example, the Latin word *habitus* means "condition" or "state," not "habit." Similarly, *familiāris* in Latin means "familiar" in the sense of being well-known but also often referred to a member of a household.

Latin is a language with a rich history, widely used throughout the Roman Empire and preserved in scholarly, religious, and legal contexts for centuries after the fall of Rome. Although no longer spoken as a native language, Latin remains indispensable for understanding classical literature, historical texts, legal terminology, and the etymology of countless modern words.

When learning a language, it's best to start with the basics and learn the most commonly used words and grammatical structures. In Latin, understanding the core vocabulary, verb conjugations, and noun declensions will help you understand the majority of Latin texts. Simply reading a word isn't going to help you remember it; rather, using it in practice exercises, translations, and memorization drills is essential for retention. Don't just skim each section in this book; spend time with each section, and use repetition to help you retain the information you're learning.

Latin requires a strong focus on grammar and structure due to its case system, which indicates the function of words in a sentence. It's crucial to understand how nouns, pronouns, and adjectives change their forms depending on their roles in a sentence. For example, *mensa* means "table" in the nominative case (subject), but *mensae* is the genitive case (of the table), showing possession.

One effective method for learning Latin vocabulary is to repeat the Latin word several times while reading it, then repeat it several times with your eyes closed. Return to the word an hour or a day later to see if you can recall its meaning and pronunciation, repeating as necessary until you know it by heart. Using flashcards, online quizzes, and translation exercises can also help reinforce your learning. It's important to consistently practice and review what you've learned to ensure long-term retention.

Unlike learning a modern language, where immersion in daily conversations or media is possible, learning Latin often involves reading and translating classical texts. However, you can still immerse yourself by reading Latin literature, inscriptions, and practicing translations regularly. The more you engage with the language, the more familiar and intuitive it will become.

At the start, Latin may seem challenging, and you might feel overwhelmed by the complexity of the grammar and the volume of vocabulary to learn. Don't worry, this is a common experience for all learners. Focus on understanding the grammar and gradually expanding your vocabulary. Over time, as you practice reading and translating, you will develop a stronger command of the language.

Personal Pronouns in Latin

Starting with Latin pronouns can significantly enhance your understanding of the language. In Latin, a personal pronoun is used to indicate the subject performing an action, such as "I" (*ego*) or "we" (*nōs*).

Latin personal pronouns differ from English in that they are often omitted in sentences, as the verb ending usually indicates the subject. However, pronouns are used for emphasis or clarity. Latin also distinguishes between different forms of "you" (*tū* for singular and informal, *vōs* for plural), and there is no distinction between formal and informal address as in some modern languages. The third-person pronouns (*is, ea, id*) can also function as demonstrative pronouns (this/that).

Repetition is key to memorization, as is time and practice! Although memorizing Latin vocabulary and grammar can be demanding, consistent practice will help you build a solid foundation. Eventually, you will be able to read and understand Latin texts with greater ease.

Essential Latin Personal Pronouns

Ego (I)
Pronunciation: [eh-goh]
Example: *Ego discipulus sum.* (I am a student).

Tū (You - singular)
Pronunciation: [too]
Example: *Tū librum habēs.* (You have a book).

Is, Ea, Id (He, She, It)
Pronunciation: [is], [eh-ah], [id]
Example: *Is cibum amat. Ea pictūram spectat.* (He likes food. She looks at the picture).

Nōs (We)
Pronunciation: [nohs]
Example: *Nōs ludimus.* (We play).

Vōs (You - plural)
Pronunciation: [wohs]
Example: *Vōs linguam Latīnam discitis.* (You learn the Latin language).

Eī, Eae, Ea (They - male or mixed group, female group, neuter)
Pronunciation: [eh-ee], [eh-ai], [eh-ah]
Example: *Eī Latīnam linguam student. Eae librōs legunt.* (They study the Latin language. They read books).

Understanding Latin Pronouns and Their Declensions

In Latin, personal pronouns are integral to understanding sentence structure and grammar. Unlike in modern Romance languages, where pronouns are often required in sentences, Latin frequently omits the subject pronoun because the verb ending typically indicates the subject. However, pronouns are used for emphasis or clarity.

Latin pronouns decline according to case, which means they change form depending on their grammatical role in the sentence (subject, direct object, indirect object, etc.). Here are the primary cases for Latin pronouns:

- **Nominative (subject):**
  Ego (I), *Tū* (You), *Is* (He), *Ea* (She), *Id* (It), *Nōs* (We), *Vōs* (You - plural), *Eī* (They - masculine/mixed), *Eae* (They - feminine), *Ea* (They - neuter).
- **Genitive (possession):**
  Meī (of me), *Tuī* (of you), *Eius* (of him/her/it), *Nostrī/Nostrum* (of us), *Vestrī/Vestrum* (of you - plural), *Eōrum* (of them - masculine/neuter), *Eārum* (of them - feminine).
- **Dative (indirect object):**
  Mihi (to/for me), *Tibi* (to/for you), *Eī* (to/for him/her/it), *Nōbīs* (to/for us), *Vōbīs* (to/for you - plural), *Eīs* (to/for them - masculine/feminine/neuter).
- **Accusative (direct object):**
  Mē (me), *Tē* (you), *Eum* (him), *Eam* (her), *Id* (it), *Nōs* (us), *Vōs* (you - plural), *Eōs* (them - masculine), *Eās* (them - feminine).
- **Ablative (means or manner):**
  Mē (by/with/from me), *Tē* (by/with/from you), *Eō* (by/with/from him/it), *Eā* (by/with/from her), *Nōbīs* (by/with/from us), *Vōbīs* (by/with/from you - plural), *Eīs* (by/with/from them - masculine/feminine/neuter).

Comparing Latin with Modern Romance Languages

Latin, as the ancestor of modern Romance languages such as Italian, Spanish, and French, provides the foundation for many grammatical structures and vocabulary found in these languages. However, there are significant differences:

1. **Pronoun Usage:**
   In Latin, pronouns are often omitted because the verb endings clearly indicate the subject. In modern Romance languages, pronouns are used more frequently, though some languages like Italian and Spanish still omit them when the subject is clear from the verb.
2. **Pronoun Forms and Cases:**
   Latin pronouns decline according to case, which affects their form depending on their role in a sentence. Modern Romance languages have largely lost this case system. For example, Latin uses different forms like *mē* (me), *mihi* (to me), and *mei* (of me), whereas in French or Italian, the pronoun "me" is used more universally with prepositions or different verbs.
3. **Gender and Number:**
   Latin pronouns retain clear distinctions in gender (masculine, feminine, neuter) and number (singular,

plural), with corresponding changes in verb and adjective agreement. In modern Romance languages, the neuter has mostly disappeared, and the gender distinctions are more straightforward.

Understanding these pronouns and their declensions is key to mastering Latin grammar. It also provides insight into the evolution of Romance languages, where simplification and loss of certain forms have resulted in the structures seen in modern Italian, Spanish, French, and others.

Each verb is grouped by its conjugation class, and one verb from each conjugation is fully conjugated in the present indicative active tense as an example.

First Conjugation Verbs (-āre)

1. **amāre** - to love
2. **vocāre** - to call
3. **laudāre** - to praise
4. **parāre** - to prepare
5. **servāre** - to save
6. **spectāre** - to watch
7. **pugnāre** - to fight
8. **cūrāre** - to care for
9. **portāre** - to carry
10. **ambulāre** - to walk
11. **narrāre** - to tell
12. **salūtāre** - to greet
13. **habitāre** - to live, dwell
14. **laborāre** - to work
15. **rogāre** - to ask
16. **vocāre** - to call
17. **orāre** - to beg, pray
18. **mandāre** - to entrust
19. **navigāre** - to sail
20. **vulnerāre** - to wound

Conjugation Example: *amāre* (to love)

- **First Person Singular:** amō (I love)
- **Second Person Singular:** amās (you love)
- **Third Person Singular:** amat (he/she/it loves)
- **First Person Plural:** amāmus (we love)
- **Second Person Plural:** amātis (you all love)

- **Third Person Plural:** amant (they love)

When you look at the Latin verb conjugations for "amāre" (to love), you'll notice that most of the forms have a long "ā" in them, but there are two forms where the "ā" becomes a short "a." Let's break down why that happens.

1. **First Person Singular: amō (I love)** - The "ō" ending shows that the action is done by "I" (first person singular). The long "ā" in "amā-" stays long because there's nothing after it that would make it change.
2. **Second Person Singular: amās (you love)** - The "s" ending tells us that the action is done by "you" (second person singular). Again, the long "ā" stays long because it's not followed by any tricky sounds that would make it shorter.
3. **Third Person Singular: amat (he/she/it loves)** - Here's where the change happens. The ending "-t" means "he," "she," or "it" (third person singular). The long "ā" shortens to "a" because Latin had a tendency to shorten vowels before certain endings like "-t." It makes the word easier to say quickly.
4. **First Person Plural: amāmus (we love)** - The "mus" ending means "we" (first person plural). The long "ā" stays because, again, there's nothing to shorten it.
5. **Second Person Plural: amātis (you all love)** - The "tis" ending means "you all" (second person plural). The long "ā" remains here as well, for the same reason as above.
6. **Third Person Plural: amant (they love)** - Just like with "amat," the long "ā" shortens to "a" before the "-nt" ending, which means "they" (third person plural). This shortening happens because it's easier to say in the flow of speech.

Here's how you can pronounce the short and long *a*:

Short *a* (ă)

- Pronunciation: The short *a* in Latin is pronounced as [a], similar to the *a* in the English word *father*, but shorter in duration. It is a brief, crisp sound and does not linger.
- Example: *amat* (ah-maht) — "he/she/it loves"
- In *amat*, both instances of *a* are short, so they are pronounced quickly and distinctly without being drawn out.

Long *ā*

- **Pronunciation:** The long *ā* in Latin is pronounced as [a:], similar to the *a* in the English word *father*, but held for a longer duration. It has a fuller, more resonant quality due to the extended sound.
- **Example:** *amāre* (ah-mah-reh) — "to love"
- In *amāre*, the first *ā* is long, so it is pronounced with more emphasis, held a bit longer to make the *ā* sound more open and resonant.

Importance of Vowel Length in Latin:

In Classical Latin, vowel length is phonemic, meaning the duration of a vowel sound can change the meaning of a word. For example:

- *liber* (with a short *i*) means "book."
- *līber* (with a long *ī*) means "free."

While vowel length in Latin primarily refers to duration rather than significant changes in vowel quality, it remains crucial for proper pronunciation and understanding. In modern Latin texts, long vowels are often marked with a macron (e.g., ā) to indicate their extended duration.

Understanding and practicing the distinction between short and long vowels will help you accurately pronounce Latin words and grasp their meaning in context.

- *amat* (ah-maht) vs. *amāmus* (ah-mah-moos)
    - In *amat*, the *a* in both syllables is short, making the word quicker to pronounce.
    - In *amāmus*, the first *a* is long, giving it a more pronounced, drawn-out sound, while the second *a* is short.

So, in summary, the long "ā" in "amāre" stays long in most forms, but it shortens to "a" in "amat" and "amant" because of the way Latin speakers naturally pronounced the language. The shortening of the long "ā" to a short "a" before the endings *-t* (third person singular) and *-nt* (third person plural) is a consistent feature across all *-āre* verbs. Here's how it works with a few more examples:

1. Vocāre (to call)

- **First Person Singular:** vocō (I call)
- **Second Person Singular:** vocās (you call)
- **Third Person Singular:** vocat (he/she/it calls) — *ā* shortens to *a*
- **First Person Plural:** vocāmus (we call)
- **Second Person Plural:** vocātis (you all call)
- **Third Person Plural:** vocant (they call) — *ā* shortens to *a*

2. Parāre (to prepare)

- **First Person Singular:** parō (I prepare)
- **Second Person Singular:** parās (you prepare)
- **Third Person Singular:** parat (he/she/it prepares) — *ā* shortens to *a*
- **First Person Plural:** parāmus (we prepare)
- **Second Person Plural:** parātis (you all prepare)
- **Third Person Plural:** parant (they prepare) — *ā* shortens to *a*

3. Labōrāre (to work)

- **First Person Singular:** labōrō (I work)
- **Second Person Singular:** labōrās (you work)
- **Third Person Singular:** labōrat (he/she/it works) — *ā* shortens to *a*
- **First Person Plural:** labōrāmus (we work)
- **Second Person Plural:** labōrātis (you all work)
- **Third Person Plural:** labōrant (they work) — *ā* shortens to *a*

This shortening happens across all verbs that belong to the first conjugation (*-āre* verbs). The vowel length changes to make the verb endings more fluid and easier to pronounce, reflecting natural patterns in Latin speech. This rule is something to keep in mind as you study more *-āre* verbs, as it will help you recognize and correctly form the various conjugations.

Second Conjugation Verbs (-ēre)

1. **vidēre** - to see
2. **monēre** - to warn
3. **habēre** - to have
4. **tenēre** - to hold
5. **terrēre** - to frighten
6. **movēre** - to move
7. **timēre** - to fear
8. **docēre** - to teach
9. **valēre** - to be strong
10. **respondēre** - to respond
11. **iacēre** - to lie down
12. **manēre** - to remain
13. **mordēre** - to bite
14. **dēbēre** - to owe, ought
15. **gaudēre** - to rejoice
16. **rīdēre** - to laugh
17. **vidēre** - to see
18. **cavēre** - to beware
19. **nocēre** - to harm
20. **tenēre** - to hold

Conjugation Example: *vidēre* (to see)

- **First Person Singular:** videō (I see)

- **Second Person Singular:** vidēs (you see)
- **Third Person Singular:** videt (he/she/it sees)
- **First Person Plural:** vidēmus (we see)
- **Second Person Plural:** vidētis (you all see)
- **Third Person Plural:** vident (they see)

Third Conjugation Verbs (-ere)

1. **dūcere** - to lead
2. **mittere** - to send
3. **legere** - to read
4. **scrībere** - to write
5. **vincere** - to conquer
6. **quaerere** - to seek
7. **petere** - to seek
8. **cōgere** - to gather, compel
9. **cēdere** - to yield
10. **currere** - to run
11. **trahere** - to drag
12. **facere** - to do, make
13. **cōgere** - to gather, compel
14. **credere** - to believe
15. **dicere** - to say, speak
16. **vivere** - to live
17. **scindere** - to cut
18. **edere** - to eat
19. **gerere** - to wear, wage
20. **defendere** - to defend

Conjugation Example: *dūcere* (to lead)

- **First Person Singular:** dūcō (I lead)
- **Second Person Singular:** dūcis (you lead)
- **Third Person Singular:** dūcit (he/she/it leads)
- **First Person Plural:** dūcimus (we lead)
- **Second Person Plural:** dūcitis (you all lead)
- **Third Person Plural:** dūcunt (they lead)

Fourth Conjugation Verbs (-īre)

1. **audīre** - to hear
2. **scīre** - to know
3. **venīre** - to come
4. **dormīre** - to sleep
5. **aperīre** - to open
6. **invenīre** - to find
7. **sentīre** - to feel
8. **finīre** - to finish
9. **custōdīre** - to guard
10. **mūnīre** - to fortify
11. **aperīre** - to open
12. **vincīre** - to bind
13. **servīre** - to serve
14. **mentīrī** - to lie
15. **sentīre** - to feel
16. **convenīre** - to meet, come together
17. **nescīre** - to not know
18. **aperīre** - to uncover
19. **aperīre** - to reveal
20. **nutrīre** - to nourish

Conjugation Example: *audīre* **(to hear)**

- **First Person Singular:** audiō (I hear)
- **Second Person Singular:** audīs (you hear)
- **Third Person Singular:** audit (he/she/it hears)
- **First Person Plural:** audīmus (we hear)
- **Second Person Plural:** audītis (you all hear)
- **Third Person Plural:** audiunt (they hear)

Summary of Latin Verb Conjugations

Latin verb conjugation is foundational to understanding the structure and meaning of sentences. By mastering these verbs across the four conjugation patterns, you'll gain the essential tools to read, translate, and understand Latin texts more effectively.

As you study these verbs, consider how they have evolved into their counterparts in modern Romance languages, noting the changes in conjugation patterns and meanings that have occurred over time. This will deepen your understanding of both the Latin language and its significant impact on modern languages.

Practical Tips for Learning Latin Verbs

- **Practice Regularly:** Regular practice with these verb conjugations will reinforce your memory and help you recall forms more quickly.
- **Use Flashcards:** Create flashcards with the infinitive on one side and the conjugated forms on the other to test your knowledge.
- **Translate Sentences:** Start translating simple Latin sentences to see how these verbs function in context.
- **Compare with Modern Languages:** If you're familiar with any Romance languages, compare the Latin verbs with their modern equivalents to see the linguistic evolution.

Most Latin verbs follow strict rules for conjugation, but there are irregular ones that do not. Latin verbs are generally conjugated based on the subject of the sentence, as well as the tense, mood, and voice of the verb. That might sound complex, but don't worry; later chapters will explain these concepts in detail. Essentially, there are many ways a verb conjugates based on whether you're discussing the present, past, future, and so on.

For Latin verbs, the basic structure involves changing the verb ending according to the subject pronoun (ego, tū, is/ea/id, nōs, vōs, eī/eae/ea). For regular verbs in the present tense, there are predictable patterns based on the verb's infinitive ending, whether it ends in -āre, -ēre, -ere, or -īre. For example, verbs typically add:

- "**-ō**" for "**ego**" (I) - example: *ego amō* (I love)
- "**-s**" for "**tū**" (you, singular) - example: *tū amās* (you love)
- "**-t**" for "**is/ea/id**" (he/she/it) - example: *is amat* (he loves)
- "**-mus**" for "**nōs**" (we) - example: *nōs amāmus* (we love)
- "**-tis**" for "**vōs**" (you, plural) - example: *vōs amātis* (you all love)
- "**-nt**" for "**eī/eae/ea**" (they) - example: *eī amant* (they love)

The stem of the verb is the part that remains when you remove the infinitive ending ("-āre," "-ēre," "-ere," or "-īre"), so *amāre* becomes *am-* with these endings added. For instance, the verb "amāre" (to love) follows the pattern: *ego amō, tū amās, is/ea/id amat, nōs amāmus, vōs amātis, eī amant*.

In Latin, the perfect tense, used to indicate completed actions, typically involves adding specific endings to the verb stem, rather than relying on an auxiliary verb as in English. For example, the perfect tense of *amāre* is formed by using the endings "-ī" for the first person singular, resulting in *amāvī* (I have loved).

The perfect tense in Latin is akin to using the simple past or present perfect in English, depending on the context. The past participle, often used to form passive constructions, is a crucial part of Latin grammar. For example, the past participle of *amāre* is *amātus* (loved). This participle can be used in various tenses, moods, and voices, making it a versatile component of Latin verb conjugation.

In Latin, unlike in modern Romance languages, the auxiliary verb *habēre* (to have) is not typically used to form the perfect tenses; instead, the perfect tense is constructed by modifying the verb itself. For instance, *amāvī* directly translates to "I have loved" without needing an auxiliary verb, reflecting Latin's more synthetic nature compared to the analytic structure of its descendants like Spanish, French, and Italian.

Understanding the Present Tense in Latin

The present tense is a grammatical tense used to describe actions, events, or states that are currently happening or that are considered general truths or facts. It's also used to describe habitual actions or routines. The present tense is one of the most commonly used tenses in many languages, including English and Latin, and it plays a crucial role in conveying messages about the present time.

Present Tense in Latin

In Latin, the present tense functions similarly to how it does in English. However, Latin uses a single present tense form to convey meanings that might require different forms in English, such as the simple present and present continuous.

Simple Present (Latin): This form is used for actions that are happening now, general truths, or habits. Unlike English, Latin does not have a separate form for actions that are currently happening; instead, it uses the same present tense form for all these situations.

- **General truth:** *Terra rotunda est.* (The Earth is round.)
- **Habit:** *Discipulus studet.* (The student studies.)
- **Action happening now:** *Sum laetus.* (I am happy.)

Present Tense Verb Conjugation in Latin

Latin verbs in the present tense conjugate according to the subject of the sentence, similar to how verbs do in English. The verb ending changes depending on the subject pronoun (ego, tū, is/ea/id, nōs, vōs, eī/eae/ea). For example, the verb *esse* (to be) is conjugated as follows:

- **First Person Singular:** *sum* (I am)
- **Second Person Singular:** *es* (you are)
- **Third Person Singular:** *est* (he/she/it is)
- **First Person Plural:** *sumus* (we are)
- **Second Person Plural:** *estis* (you all are)
- **Third Person Plural:** *sunt* (they are)

In English, verbs do not always change form based on the subject, except for the third person singular (e.g., *I run* vs. *he runs*). In Latin, however, the verb endings change more consistently to match the subject pronoun. For instance, *sum* means "I am," while *est* means "he/she/it is."

This single present tense form in Latin can express a range of meanings depending on the context, making it a versatile and essential part of the language. This is similar to how in Italian or Spanish (both Romance languages derived from Latin), a single present tense form is used for various situations that in English might require different forms. For example, the Italian *io sono* and the Spanish *yo soy* both mean "I am," reflecting the Latin *sum*.

Understanding these basic present tense forms in Latin is crucial for reading and translating Latin texts, as it lays the foundation for more complex grammatical structures.

An auxiliary verb, often referred to as a "helping verb," is a verb that works alongside the main verb in a sentence to form various tenses, moods, or voices. These verbs are crucial for constructing compound verb forms, allowing speakers to express more complex ideas about time, modality, and aspect. In English, common auxiliary verbs include "to be," "to have," and "to do." These help form complex tenses, as well as negations and questions.

For example:

- "To be" is used in forming continuous tenses: *I am going.*
- "To have" is used in forming perfect tenses: *I have eaten.*
- "To do" is used for forming questions and negations: *Do you know?* or *I do not understand.*

In Latin, auxiliary verbs are less commonly used in the same way they are in modern Romance languages. Instead, Latin relies heavily on inflection—the modification of the verb form itself—to indicate tense, mood, or voice. This means Latin can express complex ideas without the need for additional helping verbs, unlike languages like English or Italian.

For instance, where Italian might use "avere" (to have) to form perfect tenses, Latin modifies the verb itself:

- **Italian:** *Ho amato* (I have loved)
- **Latin:** *Amāvī* (I have loved)

In Italian, the auxiliary verbs "avere" (to have) and "essere" (to be) are crucial for forming compound tenses. For example:

- *Ho finito.* (I have finished.) - Present Perfect
    - **Latin equivalent:** *Fīnīvī* (I have finished)
- *Avevamo mangiato.* (We had eaten.) - Past Perfect
    - **Latin equivalent:** *Mānsimus* (We had eaten)

"Essere" is used with verbs that express movement or changes of state, as well as for forming the passive voice:

- *Sono andato.* (I have gone.) - Present Perfect
    - **Latin equivalent:** *Īvī* (I have gone)
- *È stata vista.* (She was seen.) - Passive Voice
    - **Latin equivalent:** *Vīsa est* (She was seen)

Italian also uses modal verbs like "potere" (can), "dovere" (must), and "volere" (want) to express modality, adding further nuances to the main verb:

- *Lei può nuotare.* (She can swim.)
    - **Latin equivalent:** *Illā potest natāre.*
- *Dovresti andare.* (You should go.)
    - **Latin equivalent:** *Dēbēs īre.*

In these examples, the Latin equivalents often involve simple verb forms rather than auxiliary verbs. Latin's inflectional nature allows for the expression of tense, mood, and voice within a single word, while Italian relies on auxiliary verbs and modal verbs to convey these nuances. This difference reflects the evolution from the more synthetic structure of Latin to the more analytic structure of its descendant languages like Italian.

Latin Participles and Conjugation Overview

In Latin, participles are versatile verb forms that can function as adjectives, convey additional information about a noun, or be used in various tenses. Latin, much like its descendant languages, has several types of participles, including the present participle, perfect passive participle, and future participle.

Present Participle (Participium Praesens)

Formation: The present participle in Latin is formed by adding "-ns" (for the nominative singular) to the present stem of the verb, with a genitive ending of "-ntis." For example, the present participle of "amāre" (to love) is "amāns, amantis," meaning "loving."

Usage:

- **As an adjective:** The present participle agrees with the noun it modifies in gender, number, and case. For example, *puer amāns* ("the loving boy").
- **In ablative absolute constructions:** It often appears in phrases like *hostibus victis* ("with the enemies having been defeated").
- **As a noun:** Sometimes the present participle is used substantively, meaning it stands alone as a noun, e.g., *amāns* ("a lover").

Perfect Passive Participle (Participium Perfectum Passivum)

Formation: The perfect passive participle is formed by taking the verb stem and adding the appropriate endings for the gender and number. For first conjugation verbs like "amāre," the perfect passive participle is "amātus, amāta, amātum," meaning "loved."

Usage:

- **In perfect passive tenses:** The perfect passive participle is used with forms of the auxiliary verb "esse" (to be) to form the perfect passive, pluperfect passive, and future perfect passive tenses. For example, *amātus sum* ("I have been loved"), *amātus eram* ("I had been loved"), *amātus erō* ("I will have been loved").
- **As an adjective:** Like the present participle, the perfect passive participle can also function as an adjective, agreeing with the noun it modifies in gender, number, and case, e.g., *fenestra fracta* ("the broken window").
- **In ablative absolute constructions:** It is also frequently used in these constructions, e.g., *urbe captā* ("with the city having been captured").

Future Participle (Participium Futurum)

Formation: The future participle is formed by adding "-ūrus, -ūra, -ūrum" to the verb stem. For example, the future participle of "amāre" is "amātūrus, amātūra, amātūrum," meaning "about to love" or "going to love."

Usage:

- **To indicate future action:** It is used to express an action that is expected to happen, often with a sense of intention or purpose, e.g., *vir amātūrus* ("the man about to love").
- **In passive periphrastic constructions:** The future participle can be combined with the verb "esse" to express necessity, e.g., *amandus est* ("he must be loved").

Comparison to Italian

In Italian, the past participle ("participio passato") is used similarly to Latin's perfect passive participle but always requires the auxiliary verbs "essere" or "avere" to form compound tenses. For instance:

- **Italian:** *Ho amato* ("I have loved")
  - **Latin equivalent:** *Amāvī* (directly meaning "I have loved" without an auxiliary)

Italian also uses the present participle ("gerundio presente") to form continuous tenses, much like English's present continuous. However, in Latin, continuous action is expressed differently, typically with the imperfect tense, not the gerundive.

- **Italian:** *Sto parlando* ("I am speaking")
  - **Latin equivalent:** *Dīcō* (present tense) or *Loquor* (present tense in a different context)

Irregular Verbs in Latin

Just as in Spanish and other Romance languages, Latin has its share of irregular verbs that do not follow standard conjugation patterns. These verbs must be memorized individually, as their forms vary significantly from the regular verb paradigms.

Here's a table with the full conjugation of key irregular Latin verbs across the major tenses (Present, Imperfect, Future, Perfect, Pluperfect, and Future Perfect).

Verb	Tense	1st Person Singular	2nd Person Singular	3rd Person Singular	1st Person Plural	2nd Person Plural	3rd Person Plural
Esse (to be)	**Present**	sum	es	est	sumus	estis	sunt
	Imperfect	eram	eras	erat	eramus	eratis	erant
	Future	ero	eris	erit	erimus	eritis	erunt
	Perfect	fui	fuisti	fuit	fuimus	fuistis	fuerunt
	Pluperfect	fueram	fueras	fuerat	fueramus	fueratis	fuerant
	Future Perfect	fuero	fueris	fuerit	fuerimus	fueritis	fuerint
Posse (to be able)	**Present**	possum	potes	potest	possumus	potestis	possunt

	Imperfect	poteram	poteras	poterat	poteramus	poteratis	poterant
	Future	potero	poteris	poterit	poterimus	poteritis	poterunt
	Perfect	potui	potuisti	potuit	potuimus	potuistis	potuerunt
	Pluperfect	potueram	potueras	potuerat	potueramus	potueratis	potuerant
	Future Perfect	potuero	potueris	potuerit	potuerimus	potueritis	potuerint
Velle (to want)	**Present**	volo	vis	vult	volumus	vultis	volunt
	Imperfect	volebam	volebas	volebat	volebamus	volebatis	volebant
	Future	volam	voles	volet	volemus	voletis	volent
	Perfect	volui	voluisti	voluit	voluimus	voluistis	voluerunt
	Pluperfect	volueram	volueras	voluerat	volueramus	volueratis	voluerant
	Future Perfect	voluero	volueris	voluerit	voluerimus	volueritis	voluerint
Nolle (to not want)	**Present**	nolo	non vis	non vult	nolumus	non vultis	nolunt
	Imperfect	nolebam	nolebas	nolebat	nolebamus	nolebatis	nolebant
	Future	nolam	noles	nolet	nolemus	noletis	nolent

	Perfect	nolui	noluisti	noluit	noluimus	noluistis	noluerunt
	Pluperfect	nolueram	nolueras	noluerat	nolueramus	nolueratis	noluerant
	Future Perfect	noluero	nolueris	noluerit	noluerimus	nolueritis	noluerint
Malle (to prefer)	Present	malo	mavis	mavult	malumus	mavultis	malunt
	Imperfect	malebam	malebas	malebat	malebamus	malebatis	malebant
	Future	malam	males	malet	malemus	maletis	malent
	Perfect	malui	maluisti	maluit	maluimus	maluistis	maluerunt
	Pluperfect	malueram	malueras	maluerat	malueramus	malueratis	maluerant
	Future Perfect	maluero	malueris	maluerit	maluerimus	malueritis	maluerint
Ferre (to bring)	Present	fero	fers	fert	ferimus	fertis	ferunt
	Imperfect	ferebam	ferebas	ferebat	ferebamus	ferebatis	ferebant
	Future	feram	feres	feret	feremus	feretis	ferent
	Perfect	tuli	tulisti	tulit	tulimus	tulistis	tulerunt
	Pluperfect	tuleram	tuleras	tulerat	tuleramus	tuleratis	tulerant

	Future Perfect	tulero	tuleris	tulerit	tulerimus	tuleritis	tulerint
Ire (to go)	**Present**	eo	is	it	imus	itis	eunt
	Imperfect	ibam	ibas	ibat	ibamus	ibatis	ibant
	Future	ibo	ibis	ibit	ibimus	ibitis	ibunt
	Perfect	ii	isti	iit	iimus	istis	ierunt
	Pluperfect	ieram	ieras	ierat	ieramus	ieratis	ierant
	Future Perfect	iero	ieris	ierit	ierimus	ieritis	ierint
Fieri (to become)	**Present**	fio	fis	fit	fimus	fitis	fiunt
	Imperfect	fiebam	fiebas	fiebat	fiebamus	fiebatis	fiebant
	Future	fiam	fies	fiet	fiemus	fietis	fient
	Perfect	factus sum	factus es	factus est	facti sumus	facti estis	facti sunt
	Pluperfect	factus eram	factus eras	factus erat	facti eramus	facti eratis	facti erant
	Future Perfect	factus ero	factus eris	factus erit	facti erimus	facti eritis	facti erunt
Dare (to give)	**Present**	do	das	dat	damus	datis	dant

	Imperfect	dabam	dabas	dabat	dabamus	dabatis	dabant
	Future	dabo	dabis	dabit	dabimus	dabitis	dabunt
	Perfect	dedi	dedisti	dedit	dedimus	dedistis	dederunt
	Pluperfect	dederam	dederas	dederat	dederamus	dederatis	dederant
	Future Perfect	dedero	dederis	dederit	dederimus	dederitis	dederint
Stare (to stand)	**Present**	sto	stas	stat	stamus	statis	stant
	Imperfect	stabam	stabas	stabat	stabamus	stabatis	stabant
	Future	stabo	stabis	stabit	stabimus	stabitis	stabunt
	Perfect	steti	stetisti	stetit	stetimus	stetistis	steterunt
	Pluperfect	steteram	steteras	steterat	steteramus	steteratis	steterant
	Future Perfect	stetero	steteris	steterit	steterimus	steteritis	steterint
Ducere (to lead)	**Present**	duco	ducis	ducit	ducimus	ducitis	ducunt
	Imperfect	ducebam	ducebas	ducebat	ducebamus	ducebatis	ducebant
	Future	ducam	duces	ducet	ducemus	ducetis	ducent

	Perfect	duxi	duxisti	duxit	duximus	duxistis	duxerunt
	Pluperfect	duxeram	duxeras	duxerat	duxeramus	duxeratis	duxerant
	Future Perfect	duxero	duxeris	duxerit	duxerimus	duxeritis	duxerint
Capere (to take)	**Present**	capio	capis	capit	capimus	capitis	capiunt
	Imperfect	capiebam	capiebas	capiebat	capiebamus	capiebatis	capiebant
	Future	capiam	capies	capiet	capiemus	capietis	capient
	Perfect	cepi	cepisti	cepit	cepimus	cepistis	ceperunt
	Pluperfect	ceperam	ceperas	ceperat	ceperamus	ceperatis	ceperant
	Future Perfect	cepero	ceperis	ceperit	ceperimus	ceperitis	ceperint
Facere (to do/make)	**Present**	facio	facis	facit	facimus	facitis	faciunt
	Imperfect	faciebam	faciebas	faciebat	faciebamus	faciebatis	faciebant
	Future	faciam	facies	faciet	faciemus	facietis	facient
	Perfect	feci	fecisti	fecit	fecimus	fecistis	fecerunt
	Pluperfect	feceram	feceras	fecerat	feceramus	feceratis	fecerant

	Future Perfect	fecero	feceris	fecerit	fecerimus	feceritis	fecerint
Dicere (to say)	**Present**	dico	dicis	dicit	dicimus	dicitis	dicunt
	Imperfect	dicebam	dicebas	dicebat	dicebamus	dicebatis	dicebant
	Future	dicam	dices	dicet	dicemus	dicetis	dicent
	Perfect	dixi	dixisti	dixit	diximus	dixistis	dixerunt
	Pluperfect	dixeram	dixeras	dixerat	dixeramus	dixeratis	dixerant
	Future Perfect	dixero	dixeris	dixerit	dixerimus	dixeritis	dixerint
Videre (to see)	**Present**	video	vides	videt	videmus	videtis	vident
	Imperfect	videbam	videbas	videbat	videbamus	videbatis	videbant
	Future	videbo	videbis	videbit	videbimus	videbitis	videbunt
	Perfect	vidi	vidisti	vidit	vidimus	vidistis	viderunt
	Pluperfect	videram	videras	viderat	videramus	videratis	viderant
	Future Perfect	videro	videris	viderit	viderimus	videritis	viderint

Tenere (to hold)	**Present**	teneo	tenes	tenet	tenemus	tenetis	tenent
	Imperfect	tenebam	tenebas	tenebat	tenebamus	tenebatis	tenebant
	Future	tenebo	tenebis	tenebit	tenebimus	tenebitis	tenebunt
	Perfect	tenui	tenuisti	tenuit	tenuimus	tenuistis	tenuerunt
	Pluperfect	tenueram	tenueras	tenuerat	tenueramus	tenueratis	tenuerant
	Future Perfect	tenuero	tenueris	tenuerit	tenuerimus	tenueritis	tenuerint
Mittere (to send)	**Present**	mitto	mittis	mittit	mittimus	mittitis	mittunt
	Imperfect	mittebam	mittebas	mittebat	mittebamus	mittebatis	mittebant
	Future	mittam	mittes	mittet	mittemus	mittetis	mittent
	Perfect	misi	misisti	misit	misimus	misistis	miserunt
	Pluperfect	miseram	miseras	miserat	miseramus	miseratis	miserant
	Future Perfect	misero	miseris	miserit	miserimus	miseritis	miserint
Credere (to believe)	**Present**	credo	credis	credit	credimus	creditis	credunt

	Imperfect	credebam	credebas	credebat	credebamus	credebatis	credebant
	Future	credam	credes	credet	credemus	credetis	credent
	Perfect	credidi	credidisti	credidit	credidimus	credidistis	crediderunt
	Pluperfect	credideram	credideras	crediderat	credideramus	credideratis	crediderant
	Future Perfect	credidero	credideris	crediderit	crediderimus	credideritis	crediderint
Tangere (to touch)	Present	tango	tangis	tangit	tangimus	tangitis	tangunt
	Imperfect	tangebam	tangebas	tangebat	tangebamus	tangebatis	tangebant
	Future	tangam	tanges	tanget	tangemus	tangetis	tangent
	Perfect	tetigi	tetigisti	tetigit	tetigimus	tetigistis	tetigerunt
	Pluperfect	tetigeram	tetigeras	tetigerat	tetigeramus	tetigeratis	tetigerant
	Future Perfect	tetigero	tetigeris	tetigerit	tetigerimus	tetigeritis	tetigerint

More Verbs To Memorize:

Latin Verb	English Meaning	Conjugation (Present Tense)

Amāre	to love	amō, amās, amat, amāmus, amātis, amant
Vidēre	to see	videō, vidēs, videt, vidēmus, vidētis, vident
Dūcere	to lead	dūcō, dūcis, dūcit, dūcimus, dūcitis, dūcunt
Audīre	to hear	audiō, audīs, audit, audīmus, audītis, audiunt
Habēre	to have	habeō, habēs, habet, habēmus, habētis, habent
Capere	to take, capture	capiō, capis, capit, capimus, capitis, capiunt
Scrībere	to write	scrībō, scrībis, scrībit, scrībimus, scrībitis, scrībunt
Vincere	to conquer	vincō, vincis, vincit, vincimus, vincitis, vincunt
Facere	to do, make	faciō, facis, facit, facimus, facitis, faciunt
Esse	to be	sum, es, est, sumus, estis, sunt
Posse	to be able	possum, potes, potest, possumus, potestis, possunt
Velle	to want	volō, vīs, vult, volumus, vultis, volunt

Ferre	to bring, bear	ferō, fers, fert, ferimus, fertis, ferunt
Ire	to go	eō, īs, it, īmus, ītis, eunt
Venīre	to come	veniō, venīs, venit, venīmus, venītis, veniunt
Mittere	to send	mittō, mittis, mittit, mittimus, mittitis, mittunt
Tollere	to lift, raise	tollō, tollis, tollit, tollimus, tollitis, tollunt
Tenēre	to hold	teneō, tenēs, tenet, tenēmus, tenētis, tenent
Reddere	to return, give back	reddō, reddis, reddit, reddimus, redditis, reddunt
Agere	to do, drive	agō, agis, agit, agimus, agitis, agunt
Nescīre	to not know	nesciō, nescīs, nescit, nescīmus, nescītis, nesciunt
Scīre	to know	sciō, scīs, scit, scīmus, scītis, sciunt
Manēre	to remain, stay	maneō, manēs, manet, manēmus, manētis, manent
Lūdere	to play	lūdō, lūdis, lūdit, lūdimus, lūditis, lūdunt

Portāre	to carry	portō, portās, portat, portāmus, portātis, portant
Vocāre	to call	vocō, vocās, vocat, vocāmus, vocātis, vocant
Dormīre	to sleep	dormiō, dormīs, dormit, dormīmus, dormītis, dormiunt
Timēre	to fear	timeō, timēs, timet, timēmus, timētis, timent
Scrībere	to write	scrībō, scrībis, scrībit, scrībimus, scrībitis, scrībunt
Legere	to read, choose	legō, legis, legit, legimus, legitis, legunt
Currere	to run	currō, curris, currit, currimus, curritis, currunt

Numbers in Latin

English	Latin	Pronunciation	Example Sentence
One	ūnus	OO-noos	Habeō ūnum librum. (I have one book.)
Two	duo	DOO-oh	Sunt duo canēs in hortō. (There are two dogs in the garden.)
Three	trēs	TRAYS	Habeō trēs amīcōs. (I have three friends.)
Four	quattuor	KWAH-too-or	Vīdit quattuor equōs. (He saw four horses.)

Five	quīnque	KWEEN-kweh	Sunt quīnque discipulī. (There are five students.)
Six	sex	SEHKS	Habeō sex ovis. (I have six sheep.)
Seven	septem	SEP-tem	Vīdit septem stēllās. (He saw seven stars.)
Eight	octō	OCK-toh	Sunt octō librī in mēnsā. (There are eight books on the table.)
Nine	novem	NOH-wem	Habeō novem ānima. (I have nine souls.)
Ten	decem	DEH-kem	Sunt decem virī in urbem. (There are ten men in the city.)
Eleven	ūndecim	OON-deh-keem	Habeō ūndecim discipulōs. (I have eleven students.)
Twelve	duodecim	DOO-oh-deh-keem	Sunt duodecim mīlitēs. (There are twelve soldiers.)
Thirteen	tredecim	TRAY-deh-keem	Sunt tredecim puerī. (There are thirteen boys.)
Fourteen	quattuordecim	KWAH-too-or-DEH-keem	Sunt quattuordecim fēminae. (There are fourteen women.)
Fifteen	quīndecim	KWEEN-deh-keem	Habeō quīndecim mālōs. (I have fifteen apples.)
Sixteen	sēdecim	SAY-deh-keem	Sunt sēdecim gladiī. (There are sixteen swords.)
Seventeen	septendecim	SEP-ten-deh-keem	Sunt septendecim mūnera. (There are seventeen gifts.)
Eighteen	duodēvīgintī	DOO-oh-DAY-wee-geen-tee	Sunt duodēvīgintī librī. (There are eighteen books.)

Nineteen	ūndēvīgintī	OON-DAY-wee-geen-tee	Sunt ūndēvīgintī magistrī. (There are nineteen teachers.)
Twenty	vīgintī	WEE-geen-tee	Sunt vīgintī puellae. (There are twenty girls.)
Twenty-one	ūnus et vīgintī	OO-noos eht WEE-geen-tee	Habeō ūnum et vīgintī equōs. (I have twenty-one horses.)
Thirty	trīgintā	TREE-geen-tah	Sunt trīgintā virī in urbe. (There are thirty men in the city.)
Forty	quadrāgintā	KWAD-rah-geen-tah	Sunt quadrāgintā puerī in lūdō. (There are forty boys in the school.)
Fifty	quīnquāgintā	KWEEN-kwah-geen-tah	Sunt quīnquāgintā mīlitēs. (There are fifty soldiers.)
Sixty	sexāgintā	SEK-sah-geen-tah	Sunt sexāgintā librī. (There are sixty books.)
Seventy	septuāgintā	SEP-too-ah-geen-tah	Sunt septuāgintā discipulī. (There are seventy students.)
Eighty	octōgintā	OK-toh-geen-tah	Sunt octōgintā agrī. (There are eighty fields.)
Ninety	nōnāgintā	NOH-nah-geen-tah	Sunt nōnāgintā mālōs. (There are ninety apples.)
Hundred	centum	KEN-toom	Sunt centum virī. (There are one hundred men.)
Thousand	mīlle	MEEL-leh	Sunt mīlle librī. (There are one thousand books.)
Million	mīlle mīlia	MEEL-leh MEE-lee-ah	Sunt mīlle mīlia populī. (There are one million people.)

Additional Notes:

Writing Numbers:

- In ancient Roman numerals, numbers were typically written using letters (e.g., I for 1, V for 5, X for 10, L for 50, C for 100, D for 500, and M for 1,000). Unlike modern numerical notation, Roman numerals do not use spaces or commas for separating thousands or indicating decimals.
- Example: 1,000 would be written as **M**, and 1,500 would be written as **MD**.

Compound Numbers:

- In Latin, numbers beyond 20 are formed by combining the tens and units. For example:
    - 21: **ūnus et vīgintī** (literally "one and twenty")
    - 22: **duo et vīgintī** ("two and twenty")
- This pattern is similar to some older forms of European languages, where the unit precedes the ten.

Time in Latin:

- The Romans used a 12-hour system, divided into *ante meridiem* (before midday) and *post meridiem* (after midday), similar to the modern AM and PM. However, they measured time using sundials and water clocks, and their hour lengths varied with the seasons.
- In formal writing, they might refer to the time of day using phrases like *prima hora* (the first hour, roughly 6 AM) or *sexta hora* (the sixth hour, roughly noon).
- Example: "It is the third hour of the day" would be written as **tertia hora diei est**.

Conjunctions in Latin

- **et** (et) - and
  Amo panem et vinum. (I love bread and wine.)
- **aut** (owt) - or
  Vis aquam aut vinum? (Do you want water or wine?)
- **sed** (sed) - but
  Veni, sed moratus sum. (I came, but I was delayed.)
- **quia** (KWEE-ah) - because
  Hic sum quia discere volo. (I am here because I want to learn.)
- **at** (at) - but (yet)
  Non est albus, at niger. (It's not white, but black.)
- **tamen** (TAH-men) - however/nevertheless
  Difficile est, tamen temptabo. (It's difficult, however, I will try.)

- **igitur** (IH-gee-toor) - therefore/so
  Pluit, igitur maneo domi. (It's raining, so I stay home.)
- **ideo** (IH-deh-oh) - therefore/that's why
  Fessus sum, ideo dormitum eo. (I am tired, that's why I go to sleep.)
- **nihilominus** (NI-hee-loh-MEE-noos) - nevertheless
  Frigus est, nihilominus egrediemur. (It's cold, nevertheless, we will go out.)
- **dum** (doom) - while/as long as
  Laboro dum cantas. (I work while you sing.)
- **antequam** (AHN-teh-kwam) - before
  Vado ad forum antequam occlusum est. (I go to the forum before it is closed.)
- **postquam** (POHST-kwam) - after
  Veni postquam laboravi. (I came after I worked.)
- **ut** (oot) - so that/in order that
  Disco ut examina superem. (I study so that I can pass the exams.)
- **si** (see) - if
  Te vocabo si mane venio. (I'll call you if I arrive early.)
- **nisi** (NIH-see) - unless/in case
  Vestem cape nisi frigus est. (Take a coat in case it's cold.)
- **quamquam** (KWAHM-kwahm) - although/even though
  Ibo, quamquam pluit. (I will go, although it's raining.)
- **ubi** (OO-bee) - when (specific event)
  Te vidi ubi venisti. (I saw you when you arrived.)
- **donec** (DOH-nek) - until/as long as
  Manebo donec revenias. (I will stay until you return.)
- **cum** (koom) - when/while
  Cum venis, laetus sum. (When you come, I am happy.)

GREETINGS

- **Hello** - Salvē (SAL-way) [to one person] / Salvēte (SAL-way-teh) [to multiple people]
- **Good morning** - Bonum mane (BOH-noom MAH-neh)
- **Good afternoon** - Bonum diem (BOH-noom DEE-em)
- **Good evening** - Bonum vesperum (BOH-noom WES-peh-room)

- **Good night** - Bonam noctem (BOH-nahm NOK-tem)

ROOMS IN A HOUSE (In Domō)

- **Kitchen** - Culīna (koo-LEE-nah)
- **Living Room** - Triclīnium (tree-KLEE-nee-oom)
- **Bedroom** - Cubiculum (koo-BEE-koo-loom)
- **Bathroom** - Latrina (lah-TREE-nah) or Balneum (BAHL-neh-oom)
- **Dining Room** - Triclīnium (tree-KLEE-nee-oom) [same as the living room, often a combined space]
- **Attic** - Subtegulārium (soob-teh-goo-LAH-ree-oom)
- **Basement** - Hypogēum (hee-po-GAY-oom)
- **Office/Study** - Tablinum (TAB-lee-noom)
- **Hallway** - Vestibulum (ves-TEE-boo-loom)

BATHROOM-RELATED WORDS

- **The bathroom** - Latrina (lah-TREE-nah) or Balneum (BAHL-neh-oom)
- **The toilet** - Latrina (lah-TREE-nah) or Forica (foh-REE-kah)
- **The sink** - Labellum (lah-BEHL-loom)
- **The bathtub** - Labrum (LAH-brum) or Alveus (AHL-vay-oos)
- **The towel** - Linteum (LIN-tay-oom)
- **The soap** - Sapo (SAH-poh)
- **The mirror** - Speculum (SPEH-koo-loom)
- **The comb** - Pecten (PEK-ten)
- **The razor** - Novacula (noh-WAH-koo-lah)
- **The sponge** - Spongia (SPON-gee-ah)
- **The nail clippers** - Forceps unguium (FOR-keps OON-gwee-oom)

SHOPPING-RELATED WORDS

- **The shop/store** - Taberna (tah-BER-nah)
- **The market** - Macellum (mah-KEL-loom)
- **The basket** - Corbis (KOR-bis)
- **The cashier** - Nummularius (noom-moo-LAH-ree-oos)
- **The cash register** - Arca (AR-kah)
- **The sale** - Venditio (wen-DIH-tee-oh)
- **The discount** - Minutio pretii (mee-NOO-tee-oh PREH-tee-ee)
- **The price** - Pretium (PREH-tee-oom)
- **The receipt** - Acceptio (ahk-SEP-tee-oh)
- **The exchange** - Permutatio (pehr-moo-TAH-tee-oh)
- **The refund** - Restitutio (res-tee-TOO-tee-oh)
- **The product** - Productum (proh-DOOK-toom)
- **The shelf** - Pegma (PEG-mah)
- **The payment** - Solutio (soh-LOO-tee-oh)

DIRECTIONAL WORDS

- **Above** - Super (SOO-pehr)
- **Below** - Infra (IN-frah)
- **Left** - Sinistra (see-NEES-trah)
- **Right** - Dextra (DEKS-trah)
- **North** - Septentriones (sep-ten-tree-OH-nes)
- **South** - Meridies (meh-REE-dee-ehs)
- **East** - Oriens (OH-ree-ens)
- **West** - Occidens (ok-KIH-dens)
- **Near** - Prope (PROH-peh)
- **Far** - Longe (LONG-geh)

- **Next to** - Juxta (YOOK-stah)
- **In front of** - Ante (AN-teh)
- **Behind** - Post (POST)
- **Between** - Inter (IN-tehr)
- **Inside** - Intus (IN-toos)
- **Outside** - Foris (FOH-ris)
- **On top of** - Supra (SOO-prah)
- **Underneath** - Subter (SOOB-tehr)
- **Across from** - Trans (TRAHNS)
- **Through** - Per (PEHR)
- **To the left** - Ad sinistram (ahd see-NEES-trahm)
- **To the right** - Ad dextram (ahd DEKS-trahm)
- **Straight ahead** - Recta (REK-tah)
- **Backwards** - Retro (REH-troh)
- **Forward** - Pro (PROH)
- **Upstairs** - Sursum (SOOR-soom)
- **Downstairs** - Deorsum (deh-OR-soom)
- **Around** - Circa (KEER-kah)
- **Over** - Super (SOO-pehr)
- **Under** - Sub (SOOB)
- **Close to** - Prope (PROH-peh)
- **Far from** - Longe ab (LONG-geh ahb)
- **To the side of** - Ad latus (ahd LAH-toos)
- **Along** - Per (PEHR)
- **Toward** - Versus (WER-soos)
- **Away from** - Ab (ahb)
- **At the end of** - In fine (in FEE-neh)
- **At the corner of** - In angulo (in AHN-goo-loh)
- **Opposite** - Contra (KON-trah)

COMMON HOUSEHOLD ITEMS (OBJECTA COMMUNIA DOMUS)

- **Bed** - Lectus (LEK-toos)
- **Sofa/Couch** - Lectus (used for reclining) (LEK-toos)
- **Table** - Mensa (MEN-sah)
- **Chair** - Sella (SEL-lah)
- **Lamp** - Lucerna (loo-KER-nah)
- **Storage Chest** - Arca (AR-kah)
- **Oven** - Fornax (FOR-naks)
- **Cooking Hearth** - Focus (FOH-koos)
- **Washing Basin** - Labrum (LAH-broom)
- **Clothes Line** - Vestis pendens (VES-tees PEN-dens)
- **Water Jug** - Urceus (UR-keh-oos)
- **Curtains** - Velum (WAY-loom)
- **Rug/Carpet** - Tapetum (TAH-peh-toom)
- **Shelf/Shelves** - Pegma/Pegmata (PEG-mah/PEG-mah-tah)
- **Mirror** - Speculum (SPEK-oo-loom)
- **Clock (Sundial)** - Solarium (soh-LAR-ee-oom)
- **Wall** - Paries (PAH-ree-ehs)
- **Window** - Fenestra (feh-NES-trah)

KITCHEN UTENSILS

- **The knife** - Cultrum (KUL-troom)
- **The fork** - Fuscinula (FOOS-kee-noo-lah)
- **The spoon** - Cochlear (koh-KLAY-ar)
- **The plate** - Patina (PAH-tee-nah)
- **The bowl** - Catillus (kah-TEE-loos)
- **The pan** - Sartago (sar-TAH-go)
- **The pot** - Ahenum (ah-HEH-noom)

Example Phrase:
Can you bring me the plate on the table?
Potesne mihi patinam in mensa afferre?
(POH-tehs-neh MEE-hee PAH-tee-nam in MEN-sah ah-FER-reh)

KITCHEN APPLIANCES

Since many modern appliances did not exist in Ancient Rome, the focus will be on more appropriate tools and methods:

- **The oven** - Fornax (FOR-naks)
- **The cooking hearth** - Focus (FOH-koos)
- **The food storage (pantry or storage room)** - Cella penaria (KEL-lah peh-NAH-ree-ah)
- **The brazier (for cooking)** - Ahenum (ah-HEH-noom)
- **The amphora (for storing liquids)** - Amphora (AM-for-ah)
- **The hand mill (for grinding grains)** - Mola manuaria (MOH-lah man-oo-AH-ree-ah)
- **The mortar and pestle** - Mortarium et pistillum (mor-TAR-ee-oom et pis-TEEL-loom)
- **The bread oven** - Pistrinum (pee-STREE-noom)

Example Phrase:
Can you grab the bread from the oven and place it on the table?
Potesne panem e fornace capere et in mensa ponere?
(POH-tehs-neh PAH-nem eh for-NAH-keh KAH-peh-reh et in MEN-sah POH-ne-reh)

Food Items

- **The bread** - *panis* (PAH-nees)
- **The cheese** - *caseus* (KAH-seh-oos)
- **The milk** - *lac* (lahk)
- **The egg** - *ovum* (OH-voom)
- **The apple** - *malum* (MAH-loom)
- **The olive** - *oliva* (oh-LEE-vah)
- **The fig** - *ficus* (FEE-koos)
- **The grape** - *uva* (OO-vah)
- **The chicken** - *gallina* (gah-LEE-nah)
- **The fish** - *piscis* (PEES-kees)
- **The vegetable** - *holus* (HOH-loos)
- **The lentil** - *lens* (lens)
- **The bean** - *faba* (FAH-bah)
- **The lettuce** - *lactuca* (lak-TOO-kah)
- **The onion** - *caepa* (KYE-pah)
- **The garlic** - *allium* (AHL-lee-oom)
- **The cucumber** - *cucumis* (KOO-koo-mees)
- **The carrot** - *carota* (kah-ROH-tah)
- **The honey** - *mel* (mehl)
- **The wine** - *vinum* (WEE-noom)
- **The water** - *aqua* (AH-kwah)
- **The vinegar** - *acetum* (ah-KAY-toom)
- **The oil** - *oleum* (OH-leh-oom)
- **The meat** - *caro* (KAH-roh)
- **The pork** - *porcina* (por-SEE-nah)
- **The lamb** - *agnus* (AHN-noos)
- **The bacon** - *laridum* (lah-REE-doom)
- **The sausage** - *lucanica* (loo-KAH-nee-kah)
- **The pea** - *pisum* (PEE-soom)
- **The date** - *dactylus* (DAHK-tee-loos)
- **The pear** - *pirum* (PEE-room)
- **The nut** - *nux* (nooks)
- **The mushroom** - *fungus* (FOON-goos)

Animals

- **The dog** - *canis* (KAH-nees)
- **The cat** - *feles* (FEH-les)
- **The bird** - *avis* (AH-wees)
- **The fish** - *piscis* (PEES-kees)
- **The horse** - *equus* (EH-kwoos)
- **The cow** - *vacca* (WAH-kah)
- **The sheep** - *ovis* (OH-wees)
- **The pig** - *sus* (soos)

- **The rabbit** - *cuniculus* (koo-NEE-koo-loos)
- **The mouse** - *mus* (moos)
- **The lion** - *leo* (LEH-oh)
- **The bear** - *ursus* (OOR-soos)
- **The snake** - *serpens* (SEHR-pens)
- **The turtle** - *testudo* (tehs-TOO-doh)
- **The deer** - *cervus* (KEHR-woos)
- **The wolf** - *lupus* (LOO-poos)
- **The fox** - *vulpes* (WOOL-pehs)
- **The eagle** - *aquila* (AH-kwee-lah)
- **The owl** - *strix* (streeks)
- **The goat** - *caper* (KAH-per)
- **The bull** - *taurus* (TOW-roos)
- **The donkey** - *asinus* (AH-see-noos)
- **The goose** - *anser* (AHN-sehr)
- **The duck** - *anas* (AH-nahs)
- **The rooster** - *gallus* (GAHL-loos)
- **The bee** - *apis* (AH-pees)

Outdoor Elements

- **The tree** - *arbor* (AHR-bor)
- **The grass** - *herba* (HER-bah)
- **The forest** - *silva* (SEEL-wah)
- **The river** - *flumen* (FLOO-men)
- **The sea** - *mare* (MAH-reh)
- **The mountain** - *mons* (mohns)
- **The flower** - *flos* (flohss)
- **The leaf** - *folium* (FOH-lee-oom)
- **The hill** - *collis* (KOH-lees)
- **The valley** - *vallis* (WAH-lees)
- **The cave** - *spelunca* (speh-LOON-kah)
- **The cliff** - *rupes* (ROO-pehs)
- **The waterfall** - *cataracta* (kah-tah-RAHK-tah)
- **The lake** - *lacus* (LAH-koos)
- **The pond** - *stagnum* (STAHG-noom)
- **The marsh/swamp** - *palus* (PAH-loos)
- **The rock** - *saxum* (SAHK-soom)
- **The boulder** - *rupes magna* (ROO-pehs MAHG-nah)
- **The pebble** - *calculus* (KAHL-koo-loos)
- **The soil** - *humus* (HOO-moos)
- **The sand** - *arena* (ah-REH-nah)
- **The gravel** - *sabulum* (SAH-boo-loom)
- **The dust** - *pulvis* (POOL-wees)
- **The mud** - *lutum* (LOO-toom)

School-Related Words

- **The school** - *ludus* (LOO-doos)
- **The teacher (male)** - *magister* (mah-GHEES-ter)
- **The teacher (female)** - *magistra* (mah-GHEES-trah)
- **The student (male)** - *discipulus* (dis-KIP-oo-loos)
- **The student (female)** - *discipula* (dis-KIP-oo-lah)
- **The classroom** - *schola* (SKOH-lah)
- **The desk** - *mensa* (MEN-sah)
- **The book** - *liber* (LEE-behr) or *volumen* (voh-LOO-men)
- **The notebook** - *codex* (KOH-deks)
- **The pen** - *stilus* (STEE-loos)
- **The homework** - *pensum* (PEN-soom)
- **The exam** - *examen* (eks-AH-men)
- **The subject** - *disciplina* (dis-KLEE-pee-nah)
- **The grade** - *nota* (NOH-tah)
- **The break** - *intermissio* (in-ter-MEES-syoh)
- **The library** - *bibliotheca* (bee-blee-oh-TEH-kah)
- **The ruler** - *regula* (REH-goo-lah)
- **The paper** - *charta* (KAR-tah)
- **The eraser** - *pumex* (POO-meks)

- **The scissors** - *forfex* (FOR-feks)
- **The assignment** - *pensum* (PEN-soom)
- **The test** - *examen* (eks-AH-men)
- **The answer** - *responsum* (reh-SPON-soom)
- **The diploma** - *diploma* (dee-PLOH-mah)
- **The tablet** - *tabula* (TAH-boo-lah)

Neighborhood-Related Words

- **The neighborhood** - *vicus* (WEE-koos)
- **The house** - *domus* (DOH-moos)
- **The apartment** - *insula* (IN-soo-lah)
- **The street** - *via* (WEE-ah)
- **The road** - *iter* (EE-tehr)
- **The sidewalk** - *semita* (SEH-mee-tah)
- **The park/garden** - *hortus* (HOR-toos)
- **The marketplace** - *forum* (FOH-room)
- **The bakery** - *pistrinum* (pees-TREE-noom)
- **The butcher shop** - *macellum* (mah-KEL-loom)
- **The school** - *ludus* (LOO-doos)
- **The library** - *bibliotheca* (bee-blee-oh-TEH-kah)
- **The café/inn** - *popina* (poh-PEE-nah)
- **The restaurant/tavern** - *taberna* (tah-BER-nah)
- **The bathhouse** - *thermae* (THER-mai)
- **The temple** - *templum* (TEM-ploom)
- **The amphitheater** - *amphitheatrum* (am-fee-THEH-ah-troom)
- **The basilica (court or public building)** - *basilica* (bah-SEE-lee-kah)
- **The bank/money changer** - *argentaria* (ar-ghen-TAR-ee-ah)
- **The post office/message service** - *cursus publicus* (KOOR-soos POO-bli-koos)
- **Guards (similar to modern police or national guard)** - *stationes* (stah-tyoh-NAYS)
- **Fire brigade** - *vigilum* (WEE-gee-loom)
- **The hospital/clinic** - *valetudinarium* (vah-lay-too-dee-NAH-ree-oom)
- **The bridge** - *pons* (PONS)
- **The fountain** - *fons* (FONS)
- **The river** - *flumen* (FLOO-men)
- **The hill** - *collis* (KOL-lis)
- **The mountain** - *mons* (MONS)
- **The forest** - *silva* (SEEL-wah)
- **The cave** - *spelunca* (speh-LOON-kah)
- **The cliff** - *rupes* (ROO-pays)
- **The island** - *insula* (IN-soo-lah)

Seasons

- **Spring** - *Ver* (wehr)
- **Summer** - *Aestas* (EYE-stahs)
- **Autumn/Fall** - *Autumnus* (ow-TOOM-noos)
- **Winter** - *Hiems* (HEE-ehms)

Months

- **January** - *Ianuarius* (yah-noo-AH-ree-oos)
- **February** - *Februarius* (feh-broo-AH-ree-oos)
- **March** - *Martius* (MAR-tee-oos)
- **April** - *Aprilis* (ah-PREE-lis)
- **May** - *Maius* (MYE-oos)
- **June** - *Iunius* (YOO-nee-oos)
- **July** - *Iulius* (YOO-lee-oos)
- **August** - *Augustus* (ow-GOOS-toos)
- **September** - *September* (sep-TEM-behr)
- **October** - *October* (ok-TOH-behr)
- **November** - *November* (noh-WEM-behr)

- **December** - *December* (deh-KEM-behr)

Days of the Week

- **Monday** - *Dies Lunae* (DEE-ehs LOO-neh)
- **Tuesday** - *Dies Martis* (DEE-ehs MAR-tees)
- **Wednesday** - *Dies Mercurii* (DEE-ehs MEHR-koo-ree-ee)
- **Thursday** - *Dies Iovis* (DEE-ehs YOH-wees)
- **Friday** - *Dies Veneris* (DEE-ehs WEH-neh-rees)
- **Saturday** - *Dies Saturni* (DEE-ehs sah-TOOR-nee)
- **Sunday** - *Dies Solis* (DEE-ehs SOH-lees)

Additional Useful Vocabulary

- **Today** - *Hodie* (HOH-dee-eh)
- **Tomorrow** - *Cras* (krahss)
- **Yesterday** - *Heri* (HEH-ree)
- **Now** - *Nunc* (noonk)
- **Later** - *Postea* (POS-teh-ah)
- **Morning** - *Mane* (MAH-neh)
- **Afternoon** - *Post meridiem* (POHS-teh meh-REE-dee-ehm)
- **Evening** - *Vesper* (WES-pehr)
- **Night** - *Nox* (nohks)

Family Members and Relationships

- **The woman** - *Mulier* (MOO-lee-er)
- **The girl** - *Puella* (PWEHL-lah)
- **The mother** - *Mater* (MAH-tehr)
- **The sister** - *Soror* (SOH-rohr)
- **The daughter** - *Filia* (FEE-lee-ah)
- **The grandmother** - *Avia* (AH-vee-ah)
- **The aunt** - *Amita* (AH-mee-tah) for paternal aunt, *Matertera* (MAH-tehr-teh-rah) for maternal aunt
- **The niece** - *Neptis* (NEHP-tees)
- **The wife** - *Uxor* (OOK-sohr)
- **The girlfriend** - Not a direct equivalent; might use *Amica* (ah-MEE-kah) meaning "female friend" in some contexts.

Clothing and Accessories

- **The dress** - *Stola* (STOH-lah) for a woman's dress
- **The skirt** - *Tunica* (TOO-nee-kah) could be used, though it's more general
- **The blouse** - *Tunica* (TOO-nee-kah) - as above, general for any undergarment
- **The handbag** - *Marsupium* (mahr-SOO-pee-oom)
- **The jewelry** - *Ornamenta* (or-nah-MEN-tah)

Body Parts

- **Eye** - *Oculus* (OH-koo-loos)
- **Ears** - *Aures* (OW-rehs)
- **Mouth** - *Os* (ohs)
- **Nose** - *Nasus* (NAH-soos)
- **Face** - *Facies* (FAH-kee-ehs)
- **Head** - *Caput* (KAH-poot)
- **Hair** - *Capillus* (kah-PEEL-loos)
- **Arm** - *Brachium* (BRAH-kee-oom)
- **Hand** - *Manus* (MAH-noos)
- **Finger** - *Digitus* (DEE-gee-toos)
- **Leg** - *Crus* (kroos)
- **Foot** - *Pes* (pehs)
- **Knee** - *Genu* (GEH-noo)
- **Back** - *Dorsum* (DOHR-soom)
- **Chest** - *Pectus* (PEK-toos)

- **Stomach** - *Venter* (WEHN-tehr)
- **Tooth** - *Dens* (dehns)
- **Tongue** - *Lingua* (LING-gwah)
- **Heart** - *Cor* (kohr)
- **Skin** - *Cutis* (KOO-tees)

Questions

- **Quis** - Who (kwis)
- **Quid** - What (kwid)
- **Quando** - When (KWAN-doh)
- **Ubi** - Where (OO-bee)
- **Cur** - Why (koor)
- **Quomodo** - How (KWOH-moh-doh)
- **Quis** - Which (kwis) *(Note: Latin often uses the same form for "who" and "which")*
- **Cuius** - Whose (KWEE-oos)
- **Quantum** - How much (KWAN-toom)
- **Quot** - How many (kwot)
- **Unde** - From where (OON-deh)
- **Quo** - Where to (kwoh)
- **Cur non** - Why not (koor nohn)
- **Quousque** - How long (kwoh-OOS-kweh)
- **Quotiens** - How often (KWOH-tee-ehns)
- **Cui bono** - What for (Kwee BOH-noh)

Relationships

- **Uxor** - Wife (OOK-sohr)
- **Maritus** - Husband (mah-REE-toos)
- **Amor** - Love (AH-mor)
- **Coniugium** - Marriage (koh-nee-YOO-gee-oom)
- **Amicitia** - Friendship (ah-mee-KEE-tee-ah)
- **Divortium** - Separation/Divorce (dee-WOHR-tee-oom)
- **Fides** - Loyalty/Faithfulness (FEE-dehs)
- **Affectio** - Affection (ah-FEK-tee-oh)
- **Amicus/Amica** - Friend (ah-MEE-koos/ah-MEE-kah)
- **Nuptiae** - Wedding (NOOP-tee-eye)
- **Basium** - Kiss (BAH-see-oom)
- **Dolor** - Sorrow/Grief (DOH-lor)
- **Solus** - Loneliness (SOH-loos)
- **Desiderium** - Longing/Yearning (deh-see-DEH-ree-oom)
- **Passio** - Passion (PAH-see-oh)
- **Animus** - Soul (AH-nee-moos)
- **Sponsalia** - Engagement (spohn-SAH-lee-ah)
- **Venustas** - Beauty/Charm (veh-NOOS-tahs)

Expressing Needs and Wants in Latin

- **Volo...** - I want... (WOH-loh...)
- **Egeo...** - I need... (EH-ge-o...)
- **Cupio...** - I desire... (KOO-pee-oh...)
- **Appeto...** - I crave... (ap-PEH-toh...)
- **Desidero...** - I long for... (deh-see-DEH-roh...)
- **Exopto...** - I yearn for... (eks-OP-toh...)
- **Opto...** - I wish for... (OP-toh...)
- **Requiro...** - I require... (reh-KWEE-roh...)
- **Insisto in...** - I insist on... (in-SEES-toh in...)
- **Postulo...** - I demand... (POS-too-loh...)
- **Expecto...** - I expect... (eks-PEK-toh...)
- **Spero...** - I hope for... (SPAY-roh...)
- **Intendo...** - I aim for... (in-TEN-doh...)
- **Quaero...** - I seek... (KWAI-roh...)
- **Nitor ad...** - I strive for... (NEE-tohr ahd...)
- **Affecto...** - I aspire to... (ah-FEK-toh...)
- **Quaerens sum...** - I am looking for... (KWAI-rens soom...)

- **Indigeo...** - I am in need of... (in-DEE-ge-oh...)
- **Cupiens sum...** - I am interested in obtaining... (KOO-pee-ens soom...)

Emergency Phrases in Latin

- **Adiūva!** - Help! (ah-DEE-oo-wah)
- **Voca vigiles!** - Call the guards/police! (WOH-kah WEE-gee-lays)
- **Mēdicum vocā!** - I need a doctor. (MAY-dee-koom WO-kah)
- **Accidēns fuit.** - There's been an accident. (ak-kee-DENS FOO-it)
- **Ignis!** - Fire! (IG-nees)
- **Siste! Fur!** - Stop! Thief! (SEES-teh FOOR)
- **Adiūva mē, quaesō!** - Help me, please! (ah-DEE-oo-wah MAY, KWAI-soh)
- **Mānsuēscē!** - Stay calm! (mahn-soo-ES-kay)
- **Exstruite aedificium!** - Evacuate the building! (eks-TROO-ee-teh aye-dee-FEE-kee-oom)
- **Sēcuritatem quaerite!** - Get to safety! (seh-KOO-ree-TAH-tem KWAI-ree-teh)
- **Ausculta mē!** - Listen to me! (ows-KOOL-tah MAY)
- **Sequere mē!** - Follow me! (SEH-kweh-reh MAY)
- **Cavē!** - Be careful! (KAH-way)
- **Caveās!** - Watch out! (kah-WEH-ahs)
- **Hīc manē!** - Stay here! (HEEK MAH-nay)
- **Recedē!** - Keep back! (reh-KEH-day)
- **Adiūvā illum/illam!** - Help him/her! (ah-DEE-oo-wah IL-loom/IL-lahm)

Colors

- **Red** - *Ruber* (ROO-behr)
- **Blue** - *Caeruleus* (kai-ROO-lay-oos)
- **Green** - *Viridis* (WIH-rih-dees)
- **Yellow** - *Flavus* (FLAH-woos)
- **Black** - *Niger* (NEE-gehr)
- **White** - *Albus* (AHL-boos)
- **Grey** - *Canus* (KAH-noos)
- **Orange** - *Aureus* (OW-ray-oos) (Though not exactly "orange," this could refer to a golden color.)
- **Pink** - *Roseus* (ROH-say-oos)
- **Purple** - *Purpureus* (poor-POO-ray-oos)
- **Brown** - *Fuscus* (FOOS-koos)
- **Beige** - *Cana* (KAH-nah) (This term was used more broadly for light colors.)
- **Turquoise** - *Caeruleus* (kai-ROO-lay-oos) (Used for blue-green hues, the same term as for blue.)
- **Gold** - *Aureus* (OW-ray-oos)
- **Silver** - *Argenteus* (ahr-GEN-tay-oos)
- **Copper** - *Aes* (AIS) (More generally for metal, but used for copper as well.)

Politics (Res Publica)

- **Government** - *Imperium* (im-PEH-ree-oom)
- **Democracy** - *Democratia* (deh-moh-KRAH-tee-ah) (Not widely used in Rome, as the system was a republic, but the term existed.)
- **Republic** - *Res Publica* (res POO-bli-kah)
- **Dictatorship** - *Dictatura* (dihk-tah-TOO-rah)
- **Election** - *Comitia* (koh-MEE-tee-ah)
- **Vote** - *Suffragium* (soof-FRAH-gee-oom)
- **Party** - *Factio* (FAHK-tee-oh)
- **Law** - *Lex* (leks)

- **Constitution** - *Constitutio* (kohn-stee-TOO-tee-oh) (Not exactly the same as modern constitutions, but used similarly.)
- **Military** - *Militia* (mee-LEE-tee-ah)
- **War** - *Bellum* (BEHL-loom)
- **Peace** - *Pax* (pahks)
- **Soldier** - *Miles* (MEE-les)
- **Weapon** - *Arma* (AHR-mah)
- **Battle** - *Pugna* (POOG-nah)
- **Strategy** - *Strategia* (strah-TEH-gee-ah)
- **Defense** - *Defensio* (deh-FEN-see-oh)
- **Attack** - *Impetus* (IM-peh-toos)
- **Victory** - *Victoria* (veek-TOH-ree-ah)
- **Defeat** - *Clades* (KLAH-des)
- **Alliance** - *Foedus* (FOH-doos)
- **Treaty** - *Pactum* (PAHK-toom)
- **Rebellion** - *Seditio* (seh-DEE-tee-oh)
- **Revolution** - *Revolutio* (reh-voh-LOO-tee-oh) (Though revolutions were rare, the concept existed.)
- **Occupation** - *Occupatio* (ohk-koo-PAH-tee-oh)
- **Resistance** - *Resistentia* (reh-see-STEN-tee-ah)
- **Espionage** - *Exploratio* (eks-ploh-RAH-tee-oh)
- **Propaganda** - *Propagatio* (proh-pah-GAH-tee-oh) (This term evolved in later Latin, but the concept existed in various forms.)

Latin does not have articles like "the" or "a" that are found in modern languages such as Spanish or English. Instead, the definiteness or indefiniteness of a noun is understood from the context or the word order in a sentence. Here's how Latin handles what would be definite and indefinite articles in other languages:

Definite Articles

In Latin, there are no direct equivalents to "the." Instead, the noun is used without an article:

- **Canis dormit.** - The dog is sleeping. (Here, "Canis" can mean "the dog" depending on the context.)
- **Femina loquitur.** - The woman is speaking. ("Femina" can mean "the woman.")

Indefinite Articles

Similarly, Latin lacks a word for "a" or "an." The noun alone often conveys the indefinite meaning:

- **Vir venit.** - A man is coming. (Here, "Vir" can mean "a man.")
- **Mulier loquitur.** - A woman is speaking. ("Mulier" can mean "a woman.")

Key Points:

- **No Articles:** Latin relies on context and word order rather than articles to convey definiteness or indefiniteness.

- **Context-Dependent:** Whether a noun is definite or indefinite in Latin depends on the context of the sentence.

This lack of articles is one of the characteristics that distinguish Latin from its Romance language descendants, which developed articles as part of their grammar.

Note on Gender and Articles in Latin

In Latin, nouns also have gender—masculine, feminine, or neuter—and this gender affects the form of the adjectives and pronouns that accompany them. However, unlike modern languages, Latin does not have articles like "el" or "la." The gender of the noun is indicated by the noun itself, and the form of the adjective or pronoun that agrees with it.

Gender and Noun Endings in Latin

1. **Masculine**: Nouns typically ending in **-us** (e.g., *servus* - "slave"), but there are exceptions.
   - Example: *Vir* (man), *puer* (boy).
2. **Feminine**: Nouns typically ending in **-a** (e.g., *puella* - "girl"), though there are exceptions.
   - Example: *Femina* (woman), *aqua* (water).
3. **Neuter**: Nouns often ending in **-um** (e.g., *bellum* - "war").
   - Example: *templum* (temple), *verbum* (word).

Example Sentences with Gender:

- **Masculine singular**: *Vir ambulat* (The man walks).
- **Feminine singular**: *Puella cantat* (The girl sings).
- **Neuter singular**: *Bellum geritur* (The war is waged).

Gender Rules and Exceptions

Similar to Spanish, while there are standard rules for gender in Latin, there are exceptions that need to be memorized. For example:

- *Agricola* (farmer) is masculine despite ending in **-a**.
- *Dies* (day) is masculine, while most nouns in the **-es** ending are feminine.

Tips for Remembering Gender in Latin:

- **-us** ending nouns are typically masculine.

- **-a** ending nouns are generally feminine, with some exceptions like *agricola*.
- **-um** ending nouns are neuter.
- **Memorize** the exceptions as you learn them, just as you would in Spanish.

Expressions of Thanks in Latin

Latin does not have a direct translation for "thank you" like "gracias" in Spanish. Instead, gratitude is often expressed with phrases like:

- *Gratias tibi ago* - I give thanks to you.
- *Maximas gratias tibi ago* - I give you great thanks.

Summary:

- Latin nouns are gendered (masculine, feminine, neuter), and this affects the forms of related words.
- There are no articles in Latin, unlike Italian, French and Spanish.
- Gender rules exist but are accompanied by numerous exceptions that require memorization.
- Gratitude in Latin is expressed differently, without a direct equivalent to "thank you."

Masculine Nouns in Latin

In Latin, nouns are categorized into three genders: masculine, feminine, and neuter. Masculine nouns typically refer to male individuals, professions, and certain objects. Understanding masculine nouns in Latin involves recognizing common endings and patterns that indicate a noun's gender.

Common Endings for Masculine Nouns:

1. **-us**: The most common ending for masculine nouns in the nominative singular form is **-us**.
   - **Dominus** (lord, master)
   - **Amicus** (friend)
   - **Servus** (slave, servant)
2. **-er**: Another common ending for masculine nouns is **-er**.
   - **Puer** (boy)
   - **Ager** (field)
   - **Magister** (teacher)
3. **-or**: Nouns ending in **-or** are typically masculine and often denote professions or roles.
   - **Imperator** (commander, emperor)
   - **Rector** (leader, guide)
   - **Labor** (work, labor)
4. **-os** and **-es**: Although less common, some masculine nouns end in **-os** or **-es**.

- **Miles** (soldier)
- **Patres** (fathers, often referring to senators or ancestors)

Categories of Masculine Nouns:

1. **Male Individuals**:
    - Nouns referring to male people or animals are generally masculine.
    - **Vir** (man)
    - **Senex** (old man)
    - **Leo** (lion)
2. **Professions and Roles**:
    - Masculine nouns often denote professions or societal roles.
    - **Rex** (king)
    - **Consul** (consul, a high-ranking official)
    - **Praetor** (praetor, a magistrate)
3. **Days of the Week**:
    - In Latin, the names of the days of the week, derived from planetary gods, are masculine.
    - **Dies Martis** (Tuesday, Mars' day)
    - **Dies Iovis** (Thursday, Jupiter's day)
4. **Months of the Year**:
    - While the names of months do not have an explicit gender in the nominative case, they are often treated as masculine when declined or used in context.
    - **Ianuarius** (January)
    - **Martius** (March)
    - **Maius** (May)
5. **Abstract Concepts and Objects**:
    - Some abstract concepts and inanimate objects are also categorized as masculine.
    - **Honor** (honor)
    - **Dolor** (pain, sorrow)
    - **Gladius** (sword)

Declension Patterns:

Masculine nouns in Latin primarily belong to the second declension, though some are in the third declension. Here's a brief look at the second declension:

- **Nominative Singular**: -us (e.g., dominus)
- **Genitive Singular**: -i (e.g., domini)
- **Dative Singular**: -o (e.g., domino)
- **Accusative Singular**: -um (e.g., dominum)

- **Ablative Singular**: **-o** (e.g., domino)
- **Nominative Plural**: **-i** (e.g., domini)

Summary:

Masculine nouns in Latin are identifiable by common endings like **-us**, **-er**, and **-or**. They include nouns referring to male individuals, professions, days of the week, and certain objects. Understanding the declension patterns of masculine nouns is crucial for correct grammar and sentence structure in Latin.

Masculine Nouns in Latin

Below are examples of common Latin masculine nouns. Practice reading and repeating them until you can easily recall their meanings.

- **Vir** (man) - [weer]
- **Pater** (father) - [pah-ter]
- **Frater** (brother) - [frah-ter]
- **Magister** (teacher) - [mah-gis-ter]
- **Amicus** (friend) - [ah-mee-koos]
- **Canis** (dog) - [kah-nis]
- **Hortus** (garden) - [hor-toos]
- **Lacus** (lake) - [lah-koos]
- **Oceanus** (ocean) - [oh-keh-ah-noos]
- **Stilus** (writing tool) - [stee-loos]
- **Monitor** (monitor) - [moh-nee-tor]
- **Frigidarium** (refrigerator) - [frih-gee-dah-ree-oom]
- **Ventus** (wind) - [ven-toos]
- **Successus** (success) - [sook-cess-oos]
- **Sonitus** (sound/noise) - [soh-nee-toos]
- **Odor** (smell) - [oh-dor]
- **Coffea** (coffee) - [koh-feh-ah]
- **Vinum** (wine) - [wee-noom]
- **Panis** (bread) - [pah-nis]
- **Saccharum** (sugar) - [sak-kah-room]
- **Sal** (salt) - [sahl]
- **Piper** (pepper) - [pee-per]
- **Oriza** (rice) - [oh-ree-zah]
- **Piscis** (fish) - [pees-kees]
- **Avis** (bird) - [ah-wees]
- **Elephas** (elephant) - [eh-leh-fahs]
- **Leo** (lion) - [leh-oh]
- **Tigris** (tiger) - [tee-grees]
- **Ursus** (bear) - [oor-soos]
- **Simia** (monkey) - [see-mee-ah]
- **Lepus** (rabbit) - [leh-poos]
- **Bufo** (toad) - [boo-foh]
- **Papilio** (butterfly) - [pah-pee-lee-oh]
- **Scarabaeus** (beetle) - [skah-rah-bah-oos]
- **Quercus** (oak tree) - [kwer-koos]
- **Arbor** (tree) - [ahr-bor]
- **Lapis** (stone/pebble) - [lah-pis]
- **Rupes** (cliff/rock) - [roo-pes]
- **Mons** (mountain) - [mohns]
- **Flumen** (river) - [floo-men]
- **Fons** (spring/well) - [fons]
- **Semita** (path) - [seh-mee-tah]
- **Forum** (market) - [foh-room]
- **Taberna** (shop/store) - [tah-ber-nah]
- **Portus** (port/harbor) - [por-toos]
- **Cavea** (theater) - [kah-veh-ah]
- **Museum** (museum) - [moo-seh-oom]
- **Ludus** (game/school) - [loo-doos]
- **Palestra** (gym) - [pah-les-trah]
- **Monumentum** (monument) - [moh-noo-men-toom]

Feminine Nouns in Latin

In Latin, feminine nouns often refer to individuals of the female sex, names of abstract concepts, and certain names of places. These nouns typically follow specific patterns, making them easier to recognize. Here's how to identify and understand them:

Specific Individuals:

- **Femina** (woman) - [feh-mee-nah]
- **Mater** (mother) - [mah-ter]
- **Soror** (sister) - [soh-ror]
- **Amica** (female friend) - [ah-mee-kah]
- **Regina** (queen) - [reh-gee-nah]

Names of Places:

Feminine nouns also include many names of places, particularly those ending in "-a." These can refer to regions, cities, and other locations.

- **Italia** (Italy) - [ee-tah-lee-ah]
- **Roma** (Rome) - [roh-mah]
- **Graecia** (Greece) - [grah-kee-ah]

Abstract Concepts and Nouns Ending in "-tio":

Abstract nouns, particularly those ending in "-tio" or "-tas," are often feminine in Latin. These nouns typically describe qualities, states, or actions.

- **Natio** (nation) - [nah-tee-oh]
- **Civitas** (state/community) - [kee-wee-tahs]
- **Libertas** (freedom) - [lee-ber-tahs]
- **Virtus** (virtue) - [weer-toos]
- **Sapientia** (wisdom) - [sah-pee-en-tee-ah]

Nouns Ending in "-a":

Many Latin feminine nouns end in "-a," especially those referring to everyday objects, professions, or roles.

- **Puella** (girl) - [pweh-lah]
- **Aqua** (water) - [ah-kwah]

- **Via** (road) - [wee-ah]
- **Domina** (mistress/lady) - [doh-mee-nah]

Recognizing Feminine Nouns:

- **Endings in "-a"**: Most feminine nouns end in "-a," especially first declension nouns.
- **Abstract nouns ending in "-tas" or "-tio"**: These endings often signal a feminine noun.
- **Specific roles or titles**: Roles such as "regina" (queen) or "domina" (lady) are typically feminine.

By paying attention to these patterns, you can more easily identify and remember feminine nouns in Latin, an essential step in mastering the language's grammar and vocabulary.

Here's a list of common feminine Latin nouns along with their meanings:

- **Femina** - woman
- **Puella** - girl
- **Mater** - mother
- **Soror** - sister
- **Amica** - female friend
- **Regina** - queen
- **Domina** - mistress, lady
- **Aqua** - water
- **Vita** - life
- **Terra** - earth, land
- **Via** - road, way
- **Domus** - house, home (note: "domus" is feminine but follows fourth declension patterns)
- **Civitas** - state, community
- **Libertas** - freedom
- **Virtus** - virtue, courage
- **Sapientia** - wisdom
- **Roma** - Rome
- **Graecia** - Greece
- **Italia** - Italy
- **Natura** - nature
- **Luna** - moon
- **Victoria** - victory
- **Fortuna** - fortune, luck
- **Gloria** - glory
- **Nox** - night (note: "nox" is feminine but follows third declension patterns)
- **Flamma** - flame
- **Stella** - star
- **Causa** - cause, reason
- **Domina** - lady, mistress
- **Poena** - punishment, penalty

Neuter nouns in Latin are unique because they do not belong to the masculine or feminine categories. They follow specific declension patterns, especially noticeable in the nominative, accusative, and vocative cases. Understanding these patterns is crucial for correctly using and translating neuter nouns in Latin.

Key Characteristics of Neuter Nouns

1. **Nominative and Accusative Cases:**

- For neuter nouns, the nominative and accusative cases are always identical. This rule applies to both singular and plural forms.
- **Example**: *templum* (temple) is the same in both the nominative and accusative cases.
2. **Plural Endings**:
    - In the plural, neuter nouns typically end in *-a* in the nominative and accusative cases.
    - **Example**: *templa* (temples) is the plural form of *templum*.
3. **Vocative Case**:
    - The vocative case, used for direct address, is identical to the nominative for neuter nouns.
    - **Example**: *bellum* (war) remains the same in both nominative and vocative cases.

Nominative Singular Endings for Neuter Nouns

Neuter nouns in Latin have distinct nominative singular endings based on their declension group. Here are the common endings:

1. **2nd Declension**:
    - Endings: *-um*
    - **Example**: *templum* (temple)
2. **3rd Declension**:
    - Endings: *-men, -us, -e, -al, -ar*
    - **Example**: *nomen* (name), *mare* (sea)
3. **4th Declension**:
    - Endings: *-u*
    - **Example**: *cornu* (horn)
4. **5th Declension**:
    - Rarely includes neuter nouns.

Examples of Common Neuter Nouns

1. **Bellum** (war)
    - Singular: *Bellum* (war)
    - Plural: *Bella* (wars)
    - **Example Sentence**: *Bellum incipit* (The war begins).
2. **Templum** (temple)
    - Singular: *Templum* (temple)
    - Plural: *Templa* (temples)
    - **Example Sentence**: *Templum sacrum est* (The temple is sacred).
3. **Nomen** (name)
    - Singular: *Nomen* (name)
    - Plural: *Nomina* (names)

- **Example Sentence**: *Nomen meum est Marcus* (My name is Marcus).
4. **Mare** (sea)
    - Singular: *Mare* (sea)
    - Plural: *Maria* (seas)
    - **Example Sentence**: *Mare tranquillum est* (The sea is calm).
5. **Cornu** (horn)
    - Singular: *Cornu* (horn)
    - Plural: *Cornua* (horns)
    - **Example Sentence**: *Cornu bucinatoris sonat* (The horn of the trumpeter sounds).
6. **Donum** (gift)
    - Singular: *Donum* (gift)
    - Plural: *Dona* (gifts)
    - **Example Sentence**: *Donum tibi do* (I give you a gift).
7. **Iter** (journey)
    - Singular: *Iter* (journey)
    - Plural: *Itinera* (journeys)
    - **Example Sentence**: *Iter longum est* (The journey is long).
8. **Verbum** (word)
    - Singular: *Verbum* (word)
    - Plural: *Verba* (words)
    - **Example Sentence**: *Verbum sapientiae* (A word of wisdom).
9. **Caput** (head)
    - Singular: *Caput* (head)
    - Plural: *Capita* (heads)
    - **Example Sentence**: *Caput dolorosum est* (The head is aching).
10. **Exemplum** (example)
    - Singular: *Exemplum* (example)
    - Plural: *Exempla* (examples)
    - **Example Sentence**: *Exemplum bonum est* (It is a good example).

- **Bellum** (war)
- **Templum** (temple)
- **Nomen** (name)
- **Mare** (sea)
- **Cornu** (horn)
- **Donum** (gift)
- **Iter** (journey)
- **Verbum** (word)
- **Caput** (head)
- **Exemplum** (example)
- **Opus** (work, task)
- **Consilium** (plan, advice)
- **Pectus** (chest, heart)
- **Regnum** (kingdom)
- **Vinum** (wine)
- **Fulmen** (thunderbolt)
- **Lumen** (light)
- **Sacrificium** (sacrifice)

- **Aurum** (gold)
- **Imperium** (empire, power)
- **Monumentum** (monument)
- **Vulnus** (wound)
- **Fatum** (fate)
- **Scelus** (crime)
- **Foedus** (treaty)
- **Munus** (duty, service)
- **Beneficium** (benefit, favor)
- **Carmen** (song, poem)
- **Mysterium** (mystery)
- **Gaudium** (joy)
- **Instrumentum** (tool, instrument)
- **Judicium** (judgment, trial)
- **Spatium** (space, distance)
- **Consortium** (partnership)
- **Cubiculum** (bedroom)
- **Fundamentum** (foundation)
- **Imperium** (command, power)
- **Periculum** (danger)
- **Servitium** (service, slavery)
- **Studium** (enthusiasm, zeal)
- **Tabernaculum** (tent)
- **Tempus** (time)
- **Testamentum** (will, testament)
- **Verum** (truth)
- **Vinculum** (bond, chain)
- **Volumen** (volume, roll)
- **Animal** (animal)
- **Brachium** (arm)
- **Collum** (neck)
- **Crimen** (charge, accusation)

Summary

Neuter nouns in Latin have distinct characteristics and endings that differentiate them from masculine and feminine nouns. Recognizing these patterns, particularly the nominative singular endings and the behavior of neuter nouns in different cases, is crucial for mastering Latin grammar and vocabulary.

Homework:

Memorize the above words. Come back, look at the English words with your hand over the Spanish ones to conceal them, and try to pull up the Spanish terms entirely from memory. Repeat until you can say them by heart simply by looking at the English term. You may want to do this with each section in this chapter as well.

Here's a list of common Latin adjectives, focusing on different qualities and attributes. These adjectives are essential for building a foundational vocabulary in Latin. Remember that Latin adjectives must agree in gender, number, and case with the nouns they describe.

- **Antiquus/Antiqua** - ancient, old
- **Bonus/Bona** - good
- **Malus/Mala** - bad, evil
- **Magnus/Magna** - great, large
- **Parvus/Parva** - small, little
- **Longus/Longa** - long

- **Brevis/Breve** - short
- **Pulcher/Pulchra** - beautiful
- **Foedus/Foeda** - ugly
- **Novus/Nova** - new
- **Celer/Celeris** - fast, swift
- **Lentus/Lenta** - slow
- **Clarus/Clara** - clear, bright
- **Obscurus/Obscura** - dark, obscure
- **Fortis/Forte** - strong, brave
- **Debilis/Debile** - weak
- **Sanus/Sana** - healthy, sound
- **Aeger/Aegra** - sick, ill
- **Fidelis/Fidele** - faithful, loyal
- **Infidelis/Infidele** - unfaithful, disloyal
- **Liber/Libera** - free
- **Servus/Serva** - enslaved, servile
- **Dives/Divitis** - rich, wealthy
- **Pauper/Pauperis** - poor
- **Altus/Alta** - high, tall, deep
- **Humilis/Humile** - low, humble
- **Sapiens/Sapientis** - wise, discerning
- **Stultus/Stulta** - foolish, stupid
- **Fidus/Fida** - faithful, loyal
- **Infidus/Infida** - unfaithful, treacherous
- **Audax/Audacis** - bold, daring
- **Timidus/Timida** - fearful, timid
- **Crudelis/Crudele** - cruel, harsh
- **Miser/Misera** - miserable, wretched
- **Laetus/Laeta** - happy, joyful
- **Tristis/Triste** - sad, sorrowful
- **Gravis/Grave** - heavy, serious
- **Levis/Leve** - light, trivial
- **Verus/Vera** - true, real
- **Falsus/Falsa** - false, deceitful

In Latin, adjectives must agree with the nouns they describe in three key aspects: gender, number, and case. This means that an adjective will change its form to match the gender (masculine, feminine, neuter), number (singular, plural), and case (nominative, genitive, dative, accusative, ablative, vocative) of the noun it is modifying.

Examples:

1. **Magnus vir** (Great man)
   - *Magnus* (great) is masculine, singular, and nominative, agreeing with *vir* (man), which is also masculine, singular, and nominative.
2. **Magna puella** (Great girl)
   - *Magna* (great) is feminine, singular, and nominative, agreeing with *puella* (girl), which is also feminine, singular, and nominative.
3. **Magnum donum** (Great gift)
   - *Magnum* (great) is neuter, singular, and nominative, agreeing with *donum* (gift), which is also neuter, singular, and nominative.
4. **Magnī virī** (Great men)
   - *Magnī* (great) is masculine, plural, and nominative, agreeing with *virī* (men), which is also masculine, plural, and nominative.
5. **Magnās puellās** (Great girls)

- *Magnās* (great) is feminine, plural, and accusative, agreeing with *puellās* (girls), which is also feminine, plural, and accusative.

Explanation in More Detail:

- **Gender Agreement**:
    - Latin nouns are classified into three genders: masculine, feminine, and neuter. The adjective must match the gender of the noun. For example, *magnus* (great) becomes *magna* when modifying a feminine noun and *magnum* when modifying a neuter noun.
- **Number Agreement**:
    - Nouns and adjectives can be singular or plural. The adjective must match the number of the noun. For instance, *magnus vir* (great man) becomes *magnī virī* (great men) when the noun changes from singular to plural.
- **Case Agreement**:
    - Latin nouns and adjectives have different forms depending on their function in the sentence, indicated by cases. The nominative case is typically used for the subject of a sentence, the accusative for the direct object, the genitive to show possession, and so on. The adjective must take the correct case form to agree with the noun. For example, *magnus* in the nominative singular masculine changes to *magnī* in the nominative plural masculine, *magnās* in the accusative plural feminine, etc.

By ensuring that adjectives agree with the nouns they modify in gender, number, and case, Latin maintains clarity in sentence structure, even when word order varies.

Adjectives in Latin, similar to those in Spanish, can also be modified to express comparisons or degrees of intensity, known as comparative and superlative degrees. Here's a concise overview of how these forms are created and used in Latin:

Degrees of Adjectives in Latin

1. **Positive Degree**:
    - The base form of the adjective, used when no comparison is made.
    - **Example**: *magnus* (big).
2. **Comparative Degree**:
    - The comparative degree is used to compare differences between two entities. It is typically formed by adding the suffix *-ior* for masculine and feminine nouns, and *-ius* for neuter nouns.
    - **Example**: *maior* (bigger) as in *domus maior est quam currus* (The house is bigger than the chariot).
3. **Superlative Degree**:

- The superlative degree is used to express the highest degree of quality among three or more entities. It is formed by adding the suffix *-issimus, -issima, -issimum* depending on the gender and number.
- **Example**: *maximus* (the biggest) as in *domus maxima est* (The house is the biggest).

Examples of Common Latin Adjectives in Different Degrees:

Positive	Comparative	Superlative	English Equivalent
bonus	melior	optimus	good, better, the best
magnus	maior	maximus	big, bigger, the biggest
parvus	minor	minimus	small, smaller, the smallest
longus	longior	longissimus	long, longer, the longest
iuvenis	iunior	adulescentissimus	young, younger, the youngest
vetus	vetustior	veterrimus	old, older, the oldest
brevis	brevior	brevissimus	short, shorter, the shortest
malus	peior	pessimus	bad, worse, the worst

calidus	calidior	calidissimus	warm, warmer, the warmest
frigidus	frigidior	frigidissimus	cold, colder, the coldest
altus	altior	altissimus	high/tall, higher/taller, the highest/tallest
clarus	clarior	clarissimus	bright, brighter, the brightest
fortis	fortior	fortissimus	strong, stronger, the strongest
gravis	gravior	gravissimus	heavy, heavier, the heaviest
levis	levior	levissimus	light, lighter, the lightest
pulcher	pulchrior	pulcherrimus	beautiful, more beautiful, the most beautiful
horridus	horridior	horridissimus	ugly, uglier, the ugliest

Latin adjectives, like those in many other languages, change form depending on whether they are being used in a positive, comparative, or superlative sense. The ability to correctly form and use these degrees is fundamental for expressing comparisons and intensities in Latin. By mastering these forms, you can more accurately convey meaning and nuance in the language.

Irregular Forms in Latin

Just like in Spanish, Latin also has irregular forms for some adjectives, especially when forming comparatives and superlatives. For example:

- **Bonus** (good), **melior** (better), **optimus** (the best)
- **Magnus** (great), **maior** (greater), **maximus** (the greatest)
- **Parvus** (small), **minor** (smaller), **minimus** (the smallest)

When to Apply Changes in Adjectives

In Latin, some adjectives, like those listed above, do not follow the standard patterns for forming comparatives and superlatives. These forms need to be memorized, as they deviate from the regular endings.

Modifying Adjectives for Intensity

Latin also has ways to express different degrees of intensity or modify adjectives. This can be done by using adverbs or specific adjective forms:

- **Valde** (very) can be used to intensify: *Valde magnus* (very great).
- **Nimis** (too) expresses excess: *Nimis magnus* (too great).
- To diminish intensity, words like **paulum** (a little) can be used: *Paulum magnus* (somewhat great).

Examples of Irregular Comparatives and Superlatives

Positive	Comparative	Superlative	English Equivalent
Bonus	Melior	Optimus	good, better, the best
Magnus	Maior	Maximus	great, greater, the greatest
Parvus	Minor	Minimus	small, smaller, the smallest
Multus	Plus	Plurimus	much, more, the most
Malus	Peior	Pessimus	bad, worse, the worst

These forms are irregular and differ significantly from the regular pattern, so memorization is key to mastering their usage.

Additional Comparatives and Superlatives in Latin

Positive	Comparative	Superlative	English Equivalent
Altus	Altior	Altissimus	high, higher, the highest
Prope	Propior	Proximus	near, nearer, the nearest
Vetulus	Senior	Senissimus	old, older, the oldest
Novus	Recentior	Novissimus	new, newer, the newest
Brevis	Brevior	Brevissimus	short, shorter, the shortest

Prepositions

- **Cum (with)**
    - **Example:** *Veni cum amico.* (I came with a friend.)
- **De (from, about, concerning)**
    - **Example:** *Liber est de historia.* (The book is about history.)
    - **Example:** *Venit de Roma.* (He comes from Rome.)
- **Ad (to, toward, near)**
    - **Example:** *Ibit ad forum.* (He will go to the forum.)
- **Prope (near)**
    - **Example:** *Prope flumen est oppidum.* (Near the river is a town.)
- **Post (after)**
    - **Example:** *Post bellum pax venit.* (After the war, peace comes.)
- **Propter (because of, on account of)**
    - **Example:** *Propter amorem patriae pugnavit.* (He fought because of love for his country.)
- **Contra (against)**
    - **Example:** *Milites contra hostes pugnant.* (The soldiers fight against the enemies.)
- **Sine (without)**

- ○ **Example:** *Sine spe sumus.* (We are without hope.)
- **Per (through, by)**
  - ○ **Example:** *Per silvam ambulamus.* (We walk through the forest.)
- **Circum (around)**
  - ○ **Example:** *Murum circum urbem aedificaverunt.* (They built a wall around the city.)
- **Super (above, over)**
  - ○ **Example:** *Aquila volat super montes.* (The eagle flies above the mountains.)
- **Sub (under, below)**
  - ○ **Example:** *Canis sub mensa dormit.* (The dog sleeps under the table.)
- **Ante (before, in front of)**
  - ○ **Example:** *Ante portam stat vir.* (A man stands in front of the gate.)
- **Inter (between, among)**
  - ○ **Example:** *Inter duos montes flumen fluit.* (A river flows between two mountains.)
- **In (in, on, into, onto)**
  - ○ **Example:** *In horto laborat.* (He works in the garden.)
  - ○ **Example:** *In urbem it.* (He goes into the city.)
- **A/Ab (from, away from)**
  - ○ **Example:** *Venit ab urbe.* (He comes from the city.)
  - ○ **Example:** *A monte descendit.* (He descends from the mountain.)
- **E/Ex (out of, from)**
  - ○ **Example:** *Ex urbe fugit.* (He fled from the city.)
  - ○ **Example:** *E silva venit.* (He comes out of the forest.)
- **Trans (across)**
  - ○ **Example:** *Trans flumen navigant.* (They sail across the river.)
- **Usque ad (up to, as far as)**
  - ○ **Example:** *Ambulavit usque ad portam.* (He walked up to the gate.)
- **Apud (at, among, near, in the presence of)**
  - ○ **Example:** *Apud amicum cenavit.* (He dined at his friend's house.)
- **Praeter (except, beyond)**
  - ○ **Example:** *Nihil praeter spem reliquit.* (He left nothing except hope.)

Usage in Context

Prepositions in Latin often govern a specific case, typically either the accusative or ablative. The case that follows a preposition can affect the meaning, such as indicating movement toward (accusative) or location within (ablative).

- **In** + accusative: *In urbem* (into the city)
- **In** + ablative: *In urbe* (in the city)

Adverbs

Adverbs in Latin, much like in other languages, are used to modify verbs, adjectives, or other adverbs. They describe how, when, where, or to what extent something happens. Below are common Latin adverbs along with their English equivalents and example sentences:

- **Celeriter (Quickly)**
  - **Example:** *Currit celeriter.* (He runs quickly.)
- **Lente (Slowly)**
  - **Example:** *Ambulat lente.* (She walks slowly.)
- **Tacite (Quietly)**
  - **Example:** *Loquitur tacite.* (They speak quietly.)
- **Fortiter (Bravely, Loudly)**
  - **Example:** *Clamat fortiter.* (He shouts loudly.)
- **Mane (Early)**
  - **Example:** *Mane surgit.* (He wakes up early.)
- **Serum (Late)**
  - **Example:** *Serum advenit.* (They arrive late.)
- **Hodie (Today)**
  - **Example:** *Hodie laboramus.* (We work today.)
- **Heri (Yesterday)**
  - **Example:** *Heri ad forum iimus.* (We went to the market yesterday.)
- **Cras (Tomorrow)**
  - **Example:** *Cras proficiscemur.* (We will depart tomorrow.)
- **Hic (Here)**
  - **Example:** *Hic manet.* (He stays here.)
- **Illic (There)**
  - **Example:** *Illic est.* (The park is there.)
- **Ubique (Everywhere)**
  - **Example:** *Ubique quaesivit.* (He looked everywhere.)
- **Nusquam (Nowhere)**
  - **Example:** *Nusquam invenio.* (I can't find it anywhere.)
- **Saepe (Often)**
  - **Example:** *Saepe libros legit.* (He often reads books.)
- **Raro (Rarely)**
  - **Example:** *Raro exit.* (We rarely go out.)
- **Statim (Immediately)**
  - **Example:** *Statim respondit.* (He responded immediately.)
- **Mox (Soon)**
  - **Example:** *Mox redit.* (She will return soon.)
- **Nunc (Now)**
  - **Example:** *Nunc discedimus.* (We are leaving now.)
- **Tum (Then)**
  - **Example:** *Cenavimus, tum ad forum iimus.* (We had dinner, then went to the market.)
- **Interdum (Sometimes)**
  - **Example:** *Interdum ludit.* (He sometimes plays.)
- **Semper (Always)**
  - **Example:** *Semper sero advenit.* (He is always late.)
- **Numquam (Never)**
  - **Example:** *Numquam vinum bibit.* (He never drinks wine.)
- **Hac nocte (Tonight)**
  - **Example:** *Hac nocte conveniemus.* (We will meet tonight.)
- **Mane (In the morning)**
  - **Example:** *Mane surgit.* (He rises in the morning.)
- **Nocte (At night)**
  - **Example:** *Nocte laborat.* (She works at night.)
- **Primum (First)**
  - **Example:** *Primum, emenda.* (First, buy it.)
- **Postea (Afterwards)**
  - **Example:** *Postea domum ibimus.* (Afterwards, we will go home.)
- **Post (After)**

- **Example:** *Post cenam dormiet.* (He will sleep after dinner.)
- **Cito (Quickly, soon)**
  - **Example:** *Cito veniet.* (He will come quickly.)
- **Iterum (Again)**
  - **Example:** *Iterum tentavit.* (He tried again.)
- **Quoque (Also)**
  - **Example:** *Ego quoque veniam.* (I will also come.)
- **Etiam (Even)**
  - **Example:** *Etiam senex venit.* (Even the old man came.)
- **Paene (Almost)**
  - **Example:** *Paene perfecit.* (He almost finished.)
- **Ibi (There)**
  - **Example:** *Ibi stat.* (He stands there.)
- **Foris (Outside)**
  - **Example:** *Foris ludit.* (He plays outside.)
- **Intus (Inside)**
  - **Example:** *Intus manet.* (He stays inside.)
- **Simul (Together)**
  - **Example:** *Simul laboramus.* (We work together.)
- **Soli (Alone)**
  - **Example:** *Soli remanet.* (He remains alone.)
- **Fortasse (Perhaps)**
  - **Example:** *Fortasse veniet.* (Perhaps he will come.)

- **Bene (Well)**
  - **Example:** *Bene scribit.* (He writes well.)
- **Male (Badly)**
  - **Example:** *Male cantat.* (He sings badly.)
- **Nuper (Recently)**
  - **Example:** *Nuper advenit.* (He arrived recently.)
- **Diu (For a long time)**
  - **Example:** *Diu manet.* (He stays for a long time.)
- **Plerumque (Mostly, generally)**
  - **Example:** *Plerumque contentus est.* (He is mostly content.)
- **Nonnumquam (Sometimes)**
  - **Example:** *Nonnumquam legitur.* (It is sometimes read.)
- **Tandem (Finally)**
  - **Example:** *Tandem pervenit.* (He finally arrived.)
- **Olim (Once, formerly)**
  - **Example:** *Olim in urbe habitavit.* (Once he lived in the city.)
- **Certe (Certainly)**
  - **Example:** *Certe hoc fecit.* (He certainly did this.)
- **Satis (Enough)**
  - **Example:** *Satis pecuniae habet.* (He has enough money.)
- **Iam (Already, now)**
  - **Example:** *Iam profectus est.* (He has already left.)

Usage in Context

Adverbs in Latin, as shown above, are versatile and can be used to modify a wide range of expressions. Whether indicating time, manner, place, or degree, they provide essential details that enhance the meaning of a sentence.

Latin adverbs, like adjectives, do not change form depending on the noun they modify, making them relatively straightforward to learn and use.

Interjections in Latin

Interjections in Latin, as in other languages, are exclamatory words or phrases used to express emotions or sudden reactions. These interjections can convey surprise, joy, pain, frustration, and other feelings. Below are some common Latin interjections along with their English equivalents:

- **Ah!** - *Ah!* (Expression of surprise or realization)
    - **Example:** *Ah! Tandem advenisti!* (Ah! You have finally arrived!)
- **Heu!** - *Alas!* (Expression of sorrow or regret)
    - **Example:** *Heu! Frater mortuus est!* (Alas! My brother is dead!)
- **Eheu!** - *Oh dear! / Alas!* (Expression of distress or regret)
    - **Example:** *Eheu! Omnia perdidi!* (Oh dear! I have lost everything!)
- **Vah!** - *Bah!* (Expression of disdain or indifference)
    - **Example:** *Vah! Non curo!* (Bah! I don't care!)
- **Euge!** - *Bravo! / Well done!* (Expression of approval or joy)
    - **Example:** *Euge! Bene fecisti!* (Bravo! You did well!)
- **Io!** - *Hooray!* (Expression of joy or triumph)
    - **Example:** *Io! Victoria nostra est!* (Hooray! The victory is ours!)
- **Heu me miserum!** - *Woe is me!* (Expression of sorrow or pity for oneself)
    - **Example:** *Heu me miserum! Fortuna me deseruit!* (Woe is me! Fortune has deserted me!)
- **Papae!** - *Wow!* (Expression of amazement or wonder)
    - **Example:** *Papae! Quam magnus est elephantus!* (Wow! How big the elephant is!)
- **O!** - *Oh!* (Expression of surprise or emphasis)
    - **Example:** *O tempora, o mores!* (Oh, the times! Oh, the manners!)
- **St!** - *Shh!* (Used to quiet someone or demand silence)
    - **Example:** *St! Audi vocem!* (Shh! Listen to the voice!)
- **Hem!** - *Hmm!* (Expression of doubt or consideration)
    - **Example:** *Hem! Hoc difficile videtur.* (Hmm! This seems difficult.)
- **Vae!** - *Woe!* (Expression of grief or distress)
    - **Example:** *Vae victis!* (Woe to the vanquished!)
- **Proh pudor!** - *For shame!* (Expression of reproach or indignation)
    - **Example:** *Proh pudor! Hoc non est dignum!* (For shame! This is not worthy!)
- **Age!** - *Come on! / Go on!* (Encouragement or urging someone to action)
    - **Example:** *Age! Non cessamus!* (Come on! Let's not delay!)
- **Heu!** - *Alas! / Woe!* (Expression of grief or sorrow)
    - **Example:** *Heu! Me miserum!* (Alas! Poor me!)

WEATHER

- **Tempestas (tem-PEST-as)** - Weather
- **Sol (sohl)** - Sun
- **Pluvia (PLOO-vee-ah)** - Rain
- **Nix (neeks)** - Snow
- **Ventus (WEN-toos)** - Wind
- **Nubes (NOO-bes)** - Cloud

- **Tempestas (tem-PEST-as)** - Storm
- **Nebula (NEB-oo-lah)** - Fog
- **Procella (pro-KEL-lah)** - Thunderstorm
- **Fulmen (FOOL-men)** - Lightning
- **Tonitrus (toh-NI-trus)** - Thunder
- **Frigus (FREE-goos)** - Cold
- **Calor (KAH-lor)** - Heat

- **Pruina (proo-EE-nah)** - Frost
- **Glacies (GLAH-kee-es)** - Ice
- **Aura (OW-rah)** - Breeze
- **Lux solis (LOOKS SOH-lis)** - Sunshine
- **Grando (GRAN-doh)** - Hail
- **Siccitudo (sik-kee-TOO-doh)** - Drought
- **Typhon (TEE-phon)** - Typhoon
- **Imber (IM-ber)** - Shower (rain)

Natural Disasters

- **Inundatio (een-oon-DAH-tee-oh)** - Flood
- **Cyclon (SEE-klon)** - Cyclone
- **Glacies lubrica (GLAH-kee-es LOO-bree-kah)** - Slipperiness/Ice
- **Incrementum aquae (in-kreh-MEN-toom AH-kwah-eh)** - High water/Flooding
- **Terremotus (teh-reh-MOH-toos)** - Earthquake
- **Tsunami (TSOO-nah-mee)** - Tsunami
- **Siccitudo (sik-kee-TOO-doh)** - Drought
- **Eruptio vulcani (eh-ROOP-tee-oh wul-KAH-nee)** - Volcanic eruption
- **Labina nivis (lah-BEE-nah NEE-vis)** - Avalanche
- **Incendium silvestre (in-KEN-dee-oom sil-WES-treh)** - Forest fire

- **Tornado (tor-NAH-doh)** - Tornado
- **Procella (pro-KEL-lah)** - Hurricane
- **Erosio terrae (eh-ROH-see-oh TEHR-rye)** - Soil erosion
- **Tempestas arenae (tem-PEST-as ah-REH-nay)** - Sandstorm
- **Aestus fervor (EHY-stus FER-wor)** - Heatwave
- **Fulgur ictus (FOOL-goor EEK-toos)** - Lightning strike
- **Grando (GRAN-doh)** - Hail
- **Lapsus terrae (LAP-soos TEHR-rye)** - Landslide
- **Tempestas nivis (tem-PEST-as NEE-vis)** - Snowstorm
- **Frigus fluctus (FREE-goos FLOO-ktoos)** - Cold wave
- **Unda tempestatis (OON-dah tem-PEST-ah-tees)** - Storm surge

More Useful Words to Memorize

Health and Medicine (Salus et Medicina)

- **Salus (SAH-loos)** - Health
- **Morbus (MOR-boos)** - Illness, Disease
- **Medicina (meh-dee-KEE-nah)** - Medicine
- **Medicus (MEH-dee-koos)** - Doctor (Male)
- **Dolor (DOH-lor)** - Pain
- **Febris (FEH-bris)** - Fever
- **Tussis (TOOS-sees)** - Cough
- **Vulnus (WOOL-noos)** - Injury
- **Sanguis (SAHN-gwees)** - Blood
- **Curatio (koo-RAH-tee-oh)** - Healing, Cure
- **Symptoma (seemp-TOH-mah)** - Symptom
- **Diagnosis (dee-ahg-NOH-sees)** - Diagnosis

Transportation (Vectura)

- **Navis (NAH-wees)** - Ship
- **Equus (EH-kwuhs)** - Horse (as a mode of transport)
- **Raeda (RAH-eh-dah)** - Carriage/Wagon
- **Portus (POR-toos)** - Harbor/Port
- **Statio (STAH-tee-oh)** - Station (for a caravan or travelers)
- **Itinera (ee-TEE-neh-rah)** - Journey/Route
- **Tessera (TES-seh-rah)** - Ticket
- **Onus (OH-noos)** - Luggage/Baggage
- **Via (WEE-ah)** - Road/Way

Sports and Leisure (Ludi et Otium)

- **Ludus (LOO-doos)** - Game/Play (general term)
- **Cursus (KOOR-soos)** - Running/Race
- **Natatio (nah-TAH-tee-oh)** - Swimming
- **Equitatio (eh-kwee-TAH-tee-oh)** - Horse Riding
- **Pugilatus (poo-gee-LAH-toos)** - Boxing
- **Palaestra (pah-LES-trah)** - Gymnasium (training grounds for sports)
- **Gladiatoria (glah-dee-ah-TOH-ree-ah)** - Gladiatorial games

Culture (Cultura)

- **Cultura (kool-TOO-rah)** - Culture
- **Festum (FES-toom)** - Festival
- **Traditio (trah-DEE-tee-oh)** - Tradition
- **Feriae (FEH-ree-eye)** - Holidays
- **Ludi (LOO-dee)** - Games (public games or spectacles)
- **Theatrum (teh-AH-troom)** - Theater
- **Musica (moo-SEE-kah)** - Music
- **Ars (ars)** - Art
- **Literatura (lee-teh-rah-TOO-rah)** - Literature
- **Museum (moo-SEH-oom)** - Museum (though the concept was different, with collections of art and knowledge)

Environment (Ambiens)

- **Ambiens (AHM-bee-ens)** - Environment
- **Conservatio (kohn-ser-VAH-tee-oh)** - Conservation
- **Aqua (AH-kwa)** - Water
- **Qualitas aquae (KWAH-lee-tahs AH-kwae)** - Water Quality

- **Aeris contaminatio (AH-eh-ris kohn-tah-mee-NAH-tee-oh)** - Air Pollution
- **Flumen (FLOO-men)** - River/Stream (important for water sources and environment)
- **Silva (SEEL-wah)** - Forest
- **Agri cultura (AH-gree kool-TOO-rah)** - Agriculture (important in Roman environmental context)
- **Natura (nah-TOO-rah)** - Nature
- **Ecosystema (eh-koh-SEE-steh-mah)** - Ecosystem

Fashion (Vestitus)

- **Vestitus (wes-TEE-toos)** - Clothing
- **Tunica (TOO-nee-kah)** - Tunic
- **Stola (STOH-lah)** - Stola (a dress worn by Roman women)
- **Calcei (KAHL-keh-eye)** - Shoes
- **Pallium (PAHL-lee-um)** - Cloak or Mantle (worn by men)
- **Lacerna (lah-KER-nah)** - Cloak (used for outerwear)
- **Cingulum (KEEN-goo-loom)** - Belt
- **Bracae (BRAH-kai)** - Trousers (worn in certain regions, not typical in Rome itself)
- **Palla (PAH-lah)** - A shawl worn by women
- **Soleae (SOH-leh-aye)** - Sandals
- **Cingulum (KEEN-goo-loom)** - Belt
- **Petasus (peh-TAH-soos)** - Hat
- **Fibula (FEE-boo-lah)** - Brooch or pin (used to fasten garments)

Art and Literature (Ars et Litterae)

- **Ars (ars)** - Art
- **Pictura (peek-TOO-rah)** - Painting
- **Sculptura (skool-TOO-rah)** - Sculpture
- **Expositio (ehk-spoh-SI-tee-oh)** - Exhibition
- **Museum (moo-SEH-oom)** - Museum
- **Litterae (LEE-teh-rah-eh)** - Literature
- **Poema (poh-EH-mah)** - Poem
- **Fabula (FAH-boo-lah)** - Story/Play
- **Musica (moo-SEE-kah)** - Music
- **Concilium (kohn-KEE-lee-oom)** - Concert
- **Orchestra (or-KEHS-trah)** - Orchestra
- **Carmen (KAHR-men)** - Song
- **Theatrum (teh-AH-troom)** - Theater
- **Artifex (AR-tee-feks)** - Artist
- **Scriptor (skreep-TOR)** - Writer

Holidays and Celebrations (Feriae et Celebrationes)

- **Feriae (FEH-ree-eye)** - Holidays/Festivals
- **Saturnalia (sah-toor-NAH-lee-ah)** - Saturnalia (a major Roman festival in December)
- **Lupercalia (loo-per-KAH-lee-ah)** - Lupercalia (a February festival of purification)
- **Floralia (flo-RAH-lee-ah)** - Floralia (a festival in honor of Flora, the goddess of flowers)
- **Vinalia (wee-NAH-lee-ah)** - Vinalia (a festival dedicated to Jupiter and Venus, related to wine)
- **Kalendae Ianuariae (ka-LEHN-dai yah-noo-AH-ree-eye)** - New Year's Day (Roman New Year's celebration)
- **Natalis Solis Invicti (nah-TAH-lees SOH-lees in-WIK-tee)** - Birth of the

- Unconquered Sun (associated with the winter solstice)
- **Dies Matronalis (DEE-ehs mah-troh-NAH-lis)** - Matronalia (Mother's Day in ancient Rome, celebrated in March)
- **Parentalia (pah-rehn-TAH-lee-ah)** - Parentalia (a festival honoring deceased ancestors)
- **Ludi (LOO-dee)** - Games or public entertainments (part of many Roman festivals)
- **Ambarvalia (am-bar-VAH-lee-ah)** - A festival of purification of fields, dedicated to Ceres
- **Feralia (feh-RAH-lee-ah)** - A festival for honoring the dead, held in February
- **Dies Natales (DEE-ehs nah-TAH-lehs)** - Birthdays (Celebrated as personal holidays)
- **Cerealia (keh-REE-ah-lee-ah)** - Festival in honor of Ceres, goddess of agriculture
- **Augurium Canarium (ow-GOO-ree-oom kah-NAH-ree-oom)** - A festival involving the sacrifice of a dog to Mars

In Latin, expressing unspecified quantities is often done through the use of partitive expressions or adjectives that convey the idea of "some," "a little," "much," or "none." Here's how these concepts would typically be conveyed in Latin:

Expressing Unspecified Quantities:

Latin uses several different forms to indicate an unspecified quantity of a substance or thing, particularly when referring to food, drink, or abstract concepts.

- **"aliquid"** (something/some): Used to express an unspecified or small amount.
- **"paulum"** (a little): Indicates a small quantity.
- **"multum"** (a lot/much): Used to express a large quantity.
- **"nihil"** (nothing/none): Used in negative contexts to indicate the absence of something.

Examples:

- **Aliquid panis** (Some bread)
- **Paulum carnis** (A little meat)
- **Multum aquae** (A lot of water)
- **Nihil lactis** (No milk)

Usage in Sentences:

- **Volo aliquid panis.** (I want some bread.)

- **Paulum carnis edi.** (I ate a little meat.)
- **Multum aquae bibit.** (He drinks a lot of water.)
- **Nihil lactis habeo.** (I have no milk.)

Negative Form in Latin:

In Latin, expressing negation with quantities can be done using the word "nihil" to indicate "nothing" or "none" of something. The structure is typically straightforward, using negation along with the partitive genitive to indicate the absence of a substance.

Examples:

- **Nihil panis volo.** (I don't want any bread.)
- **Ea nihil insalatae comedit.** (She doesn't eat any salad.)
- **Ille nihil aquae bibit.** (He doesn't drink any water.)
- **Nihil fructuum emimus.** (We didn't buy any fruits.)

Expressions of Quantity in Latin:

Latin uses specific terms to express varying amounts of something, often using the genitive case to specify the quantity of the noun.

Examples:

- **Multum panis** (A lot of bread)
- **Paulum sacchari** (A little sugar)
- **Nimis operis** (Too much work)

Special Cases in Latin:

In Latin, when referring to quantities or parts of a group, the genitive case is often employed to denote part of a whole.

Examples:

- **Multi eorum** (Many of them)
- **Maior pars discipulorum** (Most of the students)
- **Maior pars casuum** (The majority of the cases)

Pronominal Verbs in Latin:

While Latin does not have reflexive verbs in the same way as French or Spanish, it uses reflexive pronouns ("se," "sibi," "suus") with verbs to indicate that the subject performs an action on itself.

Examples:

- **Se lavat** (He/She washes himself/herself)
- **Sibi parat** (He/She prepares something for himself/herself)
- **Suam culpam agnoscit** (He/She acknowledges his/her own fault)

Reflexive Pronouns in Latin:

In Latin, reflexive pronouns are used similarly to indicate that the subject of the verb is also the object of the action. These pronouns adjust according to the person and number but remain consistent in their function:

- **Me** (myself)
- **Te** (yourself - singular)
- **Se** (himself, herself, itself, themselves)
- **Nos** (ourselves)
- **Vos** (yourselves - plural)
- **Se** (yourself - formal, yourselves)

Examples of Common Pronominal Verbs in Latin:

While Latin doesn't have "pronominal verbs" in the same sense as modern Romance languages, it uses reflexive constructions to express actions directed back at the subject.

- **Surgere** (to get up) - Example: **Me surgo.** (I get up.)
- **Lavare** (to wash oneself) - Example: **Se lavat.** (He/She washes himself/herself.)
- **Vestire** (to get dressed) - Example: **Nos vestimus.** (We get dressed.)
- **Dentibus purgare** (to brush one's teeth) - Example: **Se dentibus purgat.** (He/She brushes his/her teeth.)
- **Cubitum ire** (to go to bed) - Example: **Se cubitum it.** (He/She goes to bed.)

Usage in Sentences:

- **Me surgo hora septima.** (I get up at seven o'clock.)
- **Ea se lavat manus.** (She washes her hands.)
- **Nos vestimus celeriter.** (We get dressed quickly.)
- **Illi se dentibus purgant.** (They brush their teeth.)
- **Vos cubitum itis mane.** (You go to bed early.)

Negative Form in Latin:

In negative sentences, the reflexive pronoun and verb are placed between the negation "non" and the verb.

- **Non me surgo mane.** (I don't get up early.)
- **Ea non se lavat saepe.** (She doesn't wash often.)
- **Nos non vestimus nunc.** (We are not getting dressed now.)
- **Illi non se dentibus purgant.** (They don't brush their teeth.)
- **Vos non cubitum itis sero.** (You don't go to bed late.)

Understanding and practicing the use of reflexive constructions in Latin is essential for accurately expressing actions that the subject performs on themselves. Regular use will help you become more comfortable with these structures in Latin.

Interrogative Forms in Latin

In Latin, questions are formed in various ways, depending on the type of question and the level of formality or emphasis desired. Here are the main methods:

1. **Simple Interrogative Particle:** Latin often uses the particle **"-ne"** attached to the first word of the sentence, usually the verb, to indicate a yes/no question.
    - **Venisne?** (Are you coming?)
2. **Using Interrogative Words:** Just like in Spanish, Latin uses specific interrogative words to ask for more detailed information. These words are typically placed at the beginning of the sentence.
    - **Quis venit?** (Who is coming?)
    - **Quid facis?** (What are you doing?)
    - **Quando venis?** (When are you coming?)
    - **Ubi vadis?** (Where are you going?)
    - **Cur ridetis?** (Why are you laughing?)
    - **Quomodo vales?** (How are you?)
    - **Quot mala vis?** (How many apples do you want?)
3. **Inversion:** In some cases, the subject follows the verb, particularly in poetry or for emphasis.
    - **Venis tu?** (Are you coming?)
4. **Using "Nonne" and "Num":**
    - **Nonne** is used when expecting a "yes" answer.
        - **Nonne venis?** (You are coming, aren't you?)
    - **Num** is used when expecting a "no" answer.
        - **Num venis?** (You aren't coming, are you?)

Common Interrogative Words in Latin:

- **Quis** (who) - **Quis venit?** (Who is coming?)
- **Quid** (what) - **Quid facis?** (What are you doing?)
- **Quando** (when) - **Quando venis?** (When are you coming?)
- **Ubi** (where) - **Ubi vadis?** (Where are you going?)
- **Cur** (why) - **Cur ridetis?** (Why are you laughing?)
- **Quomodo** (how) - **Quomodo vales?** (How are you?)
- **Quot** (how much/many) - **Quot mala vis?** (How many apples do you want?)

Summary:

In Latin, forming questions involves the use of interrogative particles, words, and sometimes inversion. Each method has its specific uses, and understanding these nuances is crucial for asking questions effectively in Latin.

Negative Structures in Latin

Negation in Latin is typically straightforward, involving the use of the word **"non"** placed before the verb. However, there are other common negative expressions and constructions that convey different nuances.

Basic Negation:

- **Non** is the most common way to negate a statement in Latin.
  - **Non loquor Anglice.** (I don't speak English.)

Other Negative Expressions:

- **Nihil** (nothing) - Used to negate something entirely.
  - **Nihil video.** (I see nothing.)
- **Nullus/nulla/nullum** (no, none) - Used to indicate the absence of something.
  - **Nullum librum habeo.** (I have no book.)
- **Nemo** (no one) - Used when referring to people.
  - **Nemo hic est.** (No one is here.)
- **Numquam** (never) - Indicates that something never happens.
  - **Numquam venit.** (He never comes.)
- **Ne... quidem** (not even) - Used for emphasis in negation.
  - **Ne unum quidem vidi.** (I didn't see even one.)
- **Nec... nec** (neither... nor) - Used to connect two negative ideas.
  - **Nec venit nec misit nuntium.** (He neither came nor sent a messenger.)

How to Make Words Plural in Latin

In Latin, forming the plural of nouns involves altering the endings based on the noun's declension and case. Here's a detailed guide on forming plurals in Latin.

First Declension (Feminine):

- **Singular Ending**: -a
- **Plural Ending**: -ae
    - **Puella** (the girl) becomes **Puellae** (the girls).
    - **Via** (the road) becomes **Viae** (the roads).

Second Declension (Masculine and Neuter):

- **Masculine Singular Ending**: -us/-er
- **Masculine Plural Ending**: -i
    - **Servus** (the slave) becomes **Servi** (the slaves).
    - **Puer** (the boy) becomes **Pueri** (the boys).
- **Neuter Singular Ending**: -um
- **Neuter Plural Ending**: -a
    - **Bellum** (the war) becomes **Bella** (the wars).
    - **Templum** (the temple) becomes **Templa** (the temples).

Third Declension (Masculine, Feminine, Neuter):

- **Masculine/Feminine Singular Ending**: Various (e.g., -is, -or)
- **Masculine/Feminine Plural Ending**: -es
    - **Rex** (the king) becomes **Reges** (the kings).
    - **Mater** (the mother) becomes **Matres** (the mothers).
- **Neuter Singular Ending**: Various (e.g., -us, -men)
- **Neuter Plural Ending**: -a
    - **Corpus** (the body) becomes **Corpora** (the bodies).
    - **Nomen** (the name) becomes **Nomina** (the names).

Fourth Declension (Mostly Masculine and Neuter):

- **Masculine Singular Ending**: -us
- **Masculine Plural Ending**: -us
    - **Manus** (the hand) becomes **Manus** (the hands).
- **Neuter Singular Ending**: -u
- **Neuter Plural Ending**: -ua

- **Cornu** (the horn) becomes **Cornua** (the horns).

Fifth Declension (Feminine):

- **Singular Ending**: -es
- **Plural Ending**: -es
    - **Res** (the thing) becomes **Res** (the things).
    - **Dies** (the day) becomes **Dies** (the days).

Here are examples of Latin noun endings with plural rules, illustrating how Latin nouns change from singular to plural:

Ending	Plural Rule	Singular Example	Plural Example
-a	1st declension feminine nouns	Puella (girl)	Puellae (girls)
-us	2nd declension masculine nouns	Servus (slave)	Servi (slaves)
-um	2nd declension neuter nouns	Bellum (war)	Bella (wars)
-is	3rd declension nouns	Rex (king)	Reges (kings)
-or	3rd declension nouns	Honor (honor)	Honores (honors)
-men	3rd declension neuter nouns	Nomen (name)	Nomina (names)
-us	4th declension masculine nouns	Manus (hand)	Manus (hands)
-u	4th declension neuter nouns	Cornu (horn)	Cornua (horns)
-es	5th declension feminine nouns	Res (thing)	Res (things)
-ies	5th declension feminine nouns	Dies (day)	Dies (days)

Key Notes:

1. **1st Declension**: Feminine nouns typically end in **-a** in the singular and **-ae** in the plural.
2. **2nd Declension**: Masculine nouns typically end in **-us** (singular) and **-i** (plural). Neuter nouns end in **-um** (singular) and **-a** (plural).
3. **3rd Declension**: Varies, with masculine and feminine nouns often taking **-es** in the plural. Neuter nouns often end in **-a** in the plural.
4. **4th Declension**: Masculine nouns have **-us** for both singular and plural, but neuter nouns use **-u** in the singular and **-ua** in the plural.
5. **5th Declension**: Feminine nouns end in **-es** for both singular and plural.

To clarify the above, Latin nouns are categorized into five different groups called declensions. Each declension has its own set of endings that change depending on the noun's role in the sentence (such as subject, object, or possession). Here's a guide to better understand the five Latin declensions:

1st Declension

- **Gender**: Mostly feminine.
- **Typical Endings**:
    - **Singular**: -a (nominative), -ae (genitive)
    - **Plural**: -ae (nominative), -arum (genitive)
- **Example**: *Puella* (girl)
    - **Singular**:
        - Nominative (subject): Puella (The girl)
        - Genitive (possession): Puellae (Of the girl)
    - **Plural**:
        - Nominative: Puellae (The girls)
        - Genitive: Puellarum (Of the girls)

2nd Declension

- **Gender**: Mostly masculine and neuter.
- **Typical Endings**:
    - **Masculine Singular**: -us (nominative), -i (genitive)
    - **Neuter Singular**: -um (nominative), -i (genitive)
    - **Masculine Plural**: -i (nominative), -orum (genitive)
    - **Neuter Plural**: -a (nominative), -orum (genitive)
- **Example (Masculine)**: *Servus* (slave)
    - **Singular**:
        - Nominative: Servus (The slave)

- - - Genitive: Servi (Of the slave)
  - - **Plural**:
      - - Nominative: Servi (The slaves)
        - Genitive: Servorum (Of the slaves)
- - **Example (Neuter)**: *Bellum* (war)
  - - **Singular**:
      - - Nominative: Bellum (The war)
        - Genitive: Belli (Of the war)
    - **Plural**:
      - - Nominative: Bella (The wars)
        - Genitive: Bellorum (Of the wars)

3rd Declension

- **Gender**: Can be masculine, feminine, or neuter.
- **Typical Endings**:
  - **Masculine/Feminine Singular**: (varied nominative endings), -is (genitive)
  - **Neuter Singular**: (varied nominative endings), -is (genitive)
  - **Masculine/Feminine Plural**: -es (nominative), -um (genitive)
  - **Neuter Plural**: -a (nominative), -um (genitive)
- **Example (Masculine)**: *Rex* (king)
  - **Singular**:
    - Nominative: Rex (The king)
    - Genitive: Regis (Of the king)
  - **Plural**:
    - Nominative: Reges (The kings)
    - Genitive: Regum (Of the kings)
- **Example (Neuter)**: *Nomen* (name)
  - **Singular**:
    - Nominative: Nomen (The name)
    - Genitive: Nominis (Of the name)
  - **Plural**:
    - Nominative: Nomina (The names)
    - Genitive: Nominum (Of the names)

4th Declension

- **Gender**: Mostly masculine, with some neuter.
- **Typical Endings**:

- - **Masculine Singular**: -us (nominative), -us (genitive)
  - **Neuter Singular**: -u (nominative), -us (genitive)
  - **Masculine Plural**: -us (nominative), -uum (genitive)
  - **Neuter Plural**: -ua (nominative), -uum (genitive)
- **Example (Masculine)**: *Manus* (hand)
  - **Singular**:
    - Nominative: Manus (The hand)
    - Genitive: Manus (Of the hand)
  - **Plural**:
    - Nominative: Manus (The hands)
    - Genitive: Manuum (Of the hands)
- **Example (Neuter)**: *Cornu* (horn)
  - **Singular**:
    - Nominative: Cornu (The horn)
    - Genitive: Cornus (Of the horn)
  - **Plural**:
    - Nominative: Cornua (The horns)
    - Genitive: Cornuum (Of the horns)

5th Declension

- **Gender**: Mostly feminine.
- **Typical Endings**:
  - **Singular**: -es (nominative), -ei (genitive)
  - **Plural**: -es (nominative), -erum (genitive)
- **Example**: *Res* (thing)
  - **Singular**:
    - Nominative: Res (The thing)
    - Genitive: Rei (Of the thing)
  - **Plural**:
    - Nominative: Res (The things)
    - Genitive: Rerum (Of the things)

Summary

- **1st Declension**: Mostly feminine, ending in **-a** in the nominative singular.
- **2nd Declension**: Masculine and neuter, ending in **-us** (masculine) or **-um** (neuter) in the nominative singular.
- **3rd Declension**: Mixed gender, varied endings in the nominative singular.

- **4th Declension**: Mostly masculine, ending in **-us** in the nominative singular.
- **5th Declension**: Mostly feminine, ending in **-es** in the nominative singular.

These patterns help you identify and use nouns correctly in Latin, depending on their function in a sentence.

CHAPTER 2: COMMON PHRASES

Common Greetings and Farewells

- **Salve!** - Hello!
- **Vale!** - Goodbye!
- **Salvete!** - Hello! (to more than one person)
- **Valete!** - Goodbye! (to more than one person)
- **Bene!** - Well! (or OK)
- **Gratias tibi ago.** - Thank you.
- **Gratias vobis ago.** - Thank you. (to more than one person)
- **Quid agis?** - How are you?
- **Bene, gratias.** - Well, thank you.
- **Et tu?** - And you?

Basic Conversations

- **Quid est nomen tibi?** - What is your name?
- **Nomen mihi est...** - My name is...
- **Unde venis?** - Where are you from?
- **Venio ex...** - I am from...
- **Quot annos natus es?** - How old are you?
- **Sum (viginti) annos natus.** - I am (twenty) years old.
- **Quid agis hodie?** - What are you doing today?
- **Ego bene sum.** - I am fine.
- **Ubi habitas?** - Where do you live?
- **Habito in...** - I live in...

Daily Activities

- **Ad scholam eo.** - I go to school.
- **Domum redeo.** - I return home.
- **Cenam parare volo.** - I want to prepare dinner.
- **Librum lego.** - I am reading a book.
- **Dormitum eo.** - I am going to sleep.
- **Sum lassus.** - I am tired.
- **Quid vis facere?** - What do you want to do?
- **Ambulare volo.** - I want to walk.
- **Cenam edere volo.** - I want to eat dinner.
- **Tempus dormire est.** - It is time to sleep.

Asking for Help

- **Auxilium!** - Help!
- **Potestne mihi auxilium dare?** - Can you help me?
- **Quomodo id facio?** - How do I do this?
- **Ubi est latrina?** - Where is the bathroom?
- **Quid significat...?** - What does ... mean?
- **Nescio.** - I don't know.
- **Veni huc.** - Come here.
- **Saepe nefas est.** - It is often wrong.
- **Fave mihi.** - Please help me.
- **Non intellego.** - I don't understand.
- **Time and Dates**
- **Hodie est...** - Today is...
- **Crastinus dies est...** - Tomorrow is...
- **Hesternus dies fuit...** - Yesterday was...
- **Quae hora est?** - What time is it?
- **Est hora...** - It is ... o'clock.
- **Mane.** - Morning.
- **Meridies.** - Noon.
- **Vespera.** - Evening.
- **Nox.** - Night.
- **Hodie est Lunae dies.** - Today is Monday.

Weather

- **Qualis est tempestas hodie?** - How is the weather today?
- **Sol lucet.** - The sun is shining.
- **Pluit.** - It is raining.
- **Ningit.** - It is snowing.
- **Frigidum est.** - It is cold.
- **Calidum est.** - It is hot.
- **Tempestas est.** - There is a storm.
- **Ventus flat.** - The wind is blowing.
- **Serenum est.** - It is clear.
- **Nubes sunt.** - There are clouds.

Numbers and Counting

- **Unus, duo, tres.** - One, two, three.
- **Quattuor, quinque, sex.** - Four, five, six.
- **Septem, octo, novem, decem.** - Seven, eight, nine, ten.
- **Undecim, duodecim, tredecim.** - Eleven, twelve, thirteen.
- **Viginti.** - Twenty.
- **Centum.** - One hundred.
- **Mille.** - One thousand.
- **Primum.** - First.
- **Secundum.** - Second.
- **Tertium.** - Third.
- **Directions**
- **Ubi est...?** - Where is...?
- **Dextra.** - Right.
- **Sinistra.** - Left.
- **Recta via.** - Straight ahead.
- **Prope.** - Near.
- **Longe.** - Far.
- **Hic.** - Here.
- **Illic.** - There.
- **Ante.** - Before, in front.
- **Post.** - After, behind.

Food and Drink

- **Esurientem sum.** - I am hungry.
- **Sitientem sum.** - I am thirsty.
- **Panem volo.** - I want bread.
- **Aquam volo.** - I want water.
- **Vinum volo.** - I want wine.
- **Fructus amo.** - I love fruit.
- **Cibus est bonus.** - The food is good.
- **Potum volo.** - I want a drink.
- **Edamus!** - Let's eat!
- **Bibamus!** - Let's drink!

Travel and Transport

- **Iter facio.** - I am traveling.
- **In urbem eo.** - I am going to the city.
- **Equo vehor.** - I ride a horse.
- **In navem ascendo.** - I board the ship.
- **Quo itis?** - Where are you going?
- **Via recta est.** - The road is straight.
- **Estne longum iter?** - Is it a long journey?
- **Cursum tenemus.** - We are on course.
- **Advenimus.** - We have arrived.
- **In via sumus.** - We are on the way.
- **School and Learning**
- **Librum lego.** - I read the book.
- **Scriptum facio.** - I write.
- **Discipulus sum.** - I am a student.
- **Magister me docet.** - The teacher teaches me.
- **Studium meum est...** - My study is...
- **Doctrina est virtus.** - Knowledge is virtue.
- **Linguam Latinam disco.** - I am learning Latin.
- **Examen habeo.** - I have an exam.
- **Litteras scribo.** - I write letters.
- **Quaestiones habeo.** - I have questions.

Asking and Answering Questions

- **Cur?** - Why?
- **Quomodo?** - How?
- **Quando?** - When?
- **Quid?** - What?
- **Ubi?** - Where?
- **Quis?** - Who?
- **Quot?** - How many?
- **Respondere possum?** - Can I answer?
- **Nescio.** - I don't know.
- **Sic.** - Yes.
- **Common Expressions and Exclamations**
- **Euge!** - Hooray!
- **O!** - Oh!
- **Heu!** - Alas!
- **Ave!** - Hail!
- **Satis!** - Enough!
- **Minime!** - No!
- **Certe!** - Certainly!
- **Quam pulchra!** - How beautiful!
- **Absit omen!** - May it not happen!
- **Valde bene!** - Very well!

Commands and Requests

- **Da mihi...** - Give me...
- **Fac hoc!** - Do this!
- **Veni huc!** - Come here!
- **Manete!** - Stay!
- **Abi!** - Go away!
- **Tace!** - Be quiet!
- **Audi me!** - Listen to me!
- **Respice!** - Look back!
- **Exspecta!** - Wait!
- **Mane!** - Stay!

Health and Well-being

- **Quomodo te habes?** - How are you feeling?
- **Bene sum.** - I am well.
- **Male sum.** - I am unwell.
- **Medicus vocandus est.** - A doctor must be called.
- **Ubi dolet?** - Where does it hurt?
- **Febrem habeo.** - I have a fever.
- **Medicamento opus est.** - I need medicine.
- **Cura te ipsum.** - Take care of yourself.
- **Valeas!** - Be well!
- **Salus sit tibi!** - Health be with you!
- **Expressing Emotions**
- **Laetus sum.** - I am happy.
- **Tristis sum.** - I am sad.
- **Iratus sum.** - I am angry.
- **Paenitet me.** - I am sorry.
- **Amor est.** - It is love.
- **Odio est.** - It is hatred.
- **Amicus sum tuus.** - I am your friend.
- **Hostis sum tuus.** - I am your enemy.
- **Gaudeo!** - I rejoice!
- **Confundor.** - I am confused.

Legal and Official Phrases

- **In iudicio.** - In court.
- **Legem sequor.** - I follow the law.
- **Vox populi.** - The voice of the people.
- **Pacta sunt servanda.** - Agreements must be kept.
- **De facto.** - In fact.
- **De iure.** - By law.
- **In absentia.** - In absence.
- **In loco parentis.** - In place of a parent.
- **Caveat emptor.** - Let the buyer beware.
- **Nulla poena sine lege.** - No penalty without a law.

Religious and Spiritual Phrases

- **Deus vult.** - God wills it.
- **Dominus vobiscum.** - The Lord be with you.
- **Pax vobiscum.** - Peace be with you.
- **In nomine Patris.** - In the name of the Father.
- **Gloria in excelsis Deo.** - Glory to God in the highest.
- **Fiat lux.** - Let there be light.
- **Memento mori.** - Remember you will die.
- **Carpe diem.** - Seize the day.
- **Credo in unum Deum.** - I believe in one God.
- **Requiescat in pace.** - Rest in peace.

Expressions of Wisdom and Learning

- **Vita brevis.** - Life is short.
- **Tempus fugit.** - Time flies.
- **Cogito, ergo sum.** - I think, therefore I am.
- **Scientia potentia est.** - Knowledge is power.
- **Amor vincit omnia.** - Love conquers all.
- **Alea iacta est.** - The die is cast.
- **Mens sana in corpore sano.** - A healthy mind in a healthy body.
- **In vino veritas.** - In wine, there is truth.
- **Fortuna favet fortibus.** - Fortune favors the brave.
- **Dum spiro, spero.** - While I breathe, I hope.

Miscellaneous Phrases

- **Sine qua non.** - An essential condition.
- **Terra incognita.** - Unknown land.
- **Persona non grata.** - An unwelcome person.
- **Status quo.** - The existing state of affairs.
- **Tabula rasa.** - A blank slate.
- **Sub rosa.** - In secret.
- **Mutatis mutandis.** - With the necessary changes.
- **Ad hoc.** - For this purpose.
- **Ad infinitum.** - To infinity.
- **Et cetera.** - And so on.

Key Regions and Countries Known to Ancient Rome

- **Italia (Italy)** - The heart of the Roman Empire, including Rome itself.
- **Gallia (Gaul)** - Modern-day France and parts of Belgium, Western Germany, and Northern Italy.
- **Germania (Germany)** - The region east of the Rhine River, inhabited by various Germanic tribes.
- **Hispania (Spain and Portugal)** - The Iberian Peninsula, including modern-day Spain and Portugal.
- **Britannia (Britain)** - The island of Great Britain, particularly the southern part, which was a Roman province.
- **Gallia Cisalpina (Northern Italy)** - The part of Gaul south of the Alps, close to Rome.
- **Gallia Transalpina (Southern France)** - The part of Gaul north of the Alps, also known as Gallia Narbonensis.
- **Aegyptus (Egypt)** - A wealthy and fertile Roman province, previously the kingdom of Cleopatra.

- **Graecia (Greece)** - The region of ancient Greek city-states, later a Roman province.
- **Asia Minor (Turkey)** - The region of modern-day Turkey, including important cities like Ephesus.
- **Syria (Syria and Lebanon)** - An important province in the eastern Roman Empire.
- **Iudaea (Judea/Palestine)** - The region around modern-day Israel, important for its Jewish population and later Christianity.
- **Armenia (Armenia)** - A kingdom often caught between Roman and Persian interests.
- **Parthia (Iran)** - A powerful empire to the east of Rome, often in conflict with Rome.
- **Dacia (Romania)** - A region north of the Danube, later conquered by Emperor Trajan.
- **Illyricum (Western Balkans)** - The region encompassing modern-day Albania, Croatia, Bosnia, and Herzegovina.
- **Mauritania (Northwest Africa)** - The region corresponding to modern-day Morocco and western Algeria.
- **Carthago (Carthage/Tunisia)** - Rome's great rival in the Punic Wars, located in North Africa.
- **Nubia (Sudan)** - The region south of Egypt, known for its powerful kingdoms.
- **Thrace (Bulgaria and Northern Greece)** - A region in the Balkans, known for its warrior tribes.
- **Mesopotamia (Iraq)** - The land between the Tigris and Euphrates, known for its ancient civilizations.
- **Arabia (Arabian Peninsula)** - The vast desert region to the southeast of the Roman Empire.
- **Scythia (Eastern Europe and Central Asia)** - The land of the nomadic Scythians, north of the Black Sea.
- **Corsica et Sardinia (Corsica and Sardinia)** - Islands west of Italy, part of the Roman Republic.
- **Cilicia (Southern Turkey)** - A coastal region in Asia Minor, known for piracy before Roman conquest.

Notable People in Ancient Rome

- **Julius Caesar** - Roman general, statesman, and key figure in the end of the Roman Republic.
- **Augustus (Octavian)** - The first Roman Emperor, founder of the Roman Empire.
- **Cleopatra VII** - The last Pharaoh of Egypt, known for her relationships with Julius Caesar and Mark Antony.
- **Mark Antony** - Roman politician and general, ally of Caesar and lover of Cleopatra.
- **Cicero** - Famous Roman orator, philosopher, and statesman.
- **Pompey the Great** - Military and political leader, part of the First Triumvirate with Caesar.
- **Nero** - Infamous Roman Emperor known for his tyrannical rule and the Great Fire of Rome.
- **Trajan** - Roman Emperor who expanded the empire to its greatest territorial extent.
- **Hadrian** - Roman Emperor known for consolidating the empire and building Hadrian's Wall in Britain.

- **Constantine the Great** - The first Christian Roman Emperor, known for founding Constantinople.
- **Spartacus** - Gladiator who led a major slave revolt against Rome.
- **Hannibal Barca** - Carthaginian general, famous for crossing the Alps to invade Italy during the Second Punic War.
- **Scipio Africanus** - Roman general who defeated Hannibal at the Battle of Zama.
- **Vercingetorix** - Gallic chieftain who led a major rebellion against Roman rule in Gaul.
- **Sulla** - Roman general and dictator who established the precedent for using military power to seize control of Rome.
- **Crassus** - Wealthy Roman general and politician, member of the First Triumvirate with Caesar and Pompey.
- **Virgil** - Roman poet, author of the "Aeneid," Rome's national epic.
- **Livy** - Roman historian, author of a monumental history of Rome.
- **Tacitus** - Roman historian known for his critical accounts of the Roman emperors.
- **Pliny the Elder** - Roman author, naturalist, and naval commander, known for his encyclopedia "Natural History."
- **Ovid** - Roman poet, famous for "Metamorphoses" and other works on love.
- **Horace** - Roman poet, known for his odes and satires.
- **Caligula** - Notoriously cruel and insane Roman Emperor.
- **Claudius** - Roman Emperor who expanded the empire by conquering Britain.
- **Tiberius** - Second Roman Emperor, known for his reclusive and paranoid later years.
- **Marcus Aurelius** - Roman Emperor and Stoic philosopher, author of "Meditations."
- **Seneca** - Roman philosopher, statesman, and tutor to Nero, known for his Stoic writings.
- **Diocletian** - Roman Emperor who restructured the empire and established the Tetrarchy.
- **Cato the Younger** - Roman statesman and Stoic philosopher, known for his opposition to Caesar.
- **Brutus** - Roman senator and one of Julius Caesar's assassins.

Occupations in Ancient Rome

- **Senator** - Senator
- **Miles** - Soldier
- **Gladiator** - Gladiator
- **Agricola** - Farmer
- **Mercator** - Merchant
- **Magister/Magistra** - Teacher (male/female)
- **Artifex** - Artisan
- **Medicus** - Doctor
- **Servus/Serva** - Slave (male/female)
- **Scriba** - Scribe
- **Sacerdos** - Priest
- **Pistor** - Baker
- **Architectus** - Architect
- **Auriga** - Charioteer
- **Fabri Ferrarii** - Blacksmith
- **Vates** - Prophet/Soothsayer
- **Poeta** - Poet
- **Lictor** - Bodyguard

- **Legatus** - Envoy/General
- **Quaestor** - Financial Administrator
- **Praetor** - Magistrate/Judge
- **Pontifex** - High Priest
- **Vinator** - Hunter
- **Viticultor** - Vine-grower/Wine Maker
- **Nauta** - Sailor
- **Negotiator** - Businessman
- **Philosophus** - Philosopher
- **Mensor** - Surveyor
- **Medicus Veterinarius** - Veterinarian
- **Faber Tignarius** - Carpenter
- **Lanista** - Trainer of Gladiators
- **Notarius** - Clerk/Scribe
- **Caupo** - Innkeeper

CHAPTER 3: GRAMMAR

3.1 Moods in Latin Grammar

In Latin, moods are used to express different attitudes towards the action of the verb. Understanding these moods is crucial for constructing accurate and meaningful sentences in Latin. Here is an overview of the main moods in Latin and how they are used.

Indicative Mood - (Modus Indicativus)

The indicative mood is used to express factual statements, descriptions of reality, and ask questions. It is the most common mood and is used for actions, events, or states that are certain or real.

Examples:

- "**Ego malum edo.**" - (I am eating an apple.)
- "**Illi in Italia habitant.**" - (They live in Italy.)

Subjunctive Mood - (Modus Subiunctivus)

The subjunctive mood is used to express doubt, potentiality, wishes, or hypothetical situations. It is often found in dependent clauses after expressions of doubt, necessity, emotion, or purpose.

Examples:

- "**Necesse est ut veniat.**" - (It is necessary that he comes.)
- "**Timeo ne veniat.**" - (I fear that he may come.)

Imperative Mood - (Modus Imperativus)

The imperative mood is used to give commands, make requests, or offer invitations. It is direct and often addressed to the second person singular or plural.

Examples:

- "**Ede malum!**" - (Eat the apple!)
- "**Venite ad forum!**" - (Come to the forum!)

Infinitive Mood - (Modus Infinitivus)

The infinitive mood is the base form of the verb and is often used as a noun or in indirect statements. In Latin, the infinitive can also function to express purpose or result.

Examples:

- **"Volo edere."** - (I want to eat.)
- **"Difficile est videre."** - (It is difficult to see.)

Participle Mood - (Modus Participialis)

Latin participles function similarly to adjectives and can describe a state of being related to the verb. Participles come in present, perfect, and future forms, and they agree in gender, number, and case with the nouns they modify.

Examples:

- **Present Participle:** "Vir currens celer est." - (The running man is fast.)
- **Perfect Participle:** "Malum editum est." - (The eaten apple is gone.)
- **Future Participle:** "Veniturus est." - (He is about to come.)

Gerund and Gerundive

Latin also features the gerund and gerundive, which are verbal nouns and adjectives, respectively, used to express necessity, purpose, or obligation.

Examples:

- **Gerund:** "Studium legendi." - (The desire of reading.)
- **Gerundive:** "Liber legendus est." - (The book must be read.)

Additional Notes:

- The subjunctive mood in Latin is essential for expressing a wide range of ideas, particularly in complex sentences involving conditions, wishes, or indirect speech.
- Latin lacks a distinct conditional mood like in some other languages, but the subjunctive can often fulfill this role, particularly in conditional sentences (e.g., "si venias, laetus sim" - If you were to come, I would be happy).
- The imperative mood in Latin can also have a future form (imperative of futurity), especially in legal or formal contexts, indicating that an action should be performed in the future.

Understanding and mastering these moods is crucial for fluency in Latin, as they allow you to express not just actions, but the nuances of possibility, necessity, and command.

3.2 Tenses in Latin Grammar

Latin verbs are conjugated to express different tenses, each of which indicates a specific time frame or aspect of an action. Below is an overview of the primary tenses used in Latin, along with specific examples of how to create each tense and what needs to be learned regarding changes in verbs or other elements.

Present Tense - (Tempus Praesens)

The present tense is used to describe actions currently happening, habitual actions, or general truths.

Example:

- **Ego edō.** - (I eat / I am eating.)

How to create: Conjugate the verb according to the subject pronoun.

Example:

- edĕre (to eat) → ego edō (I eat)

Key Changes: Learn the present tense conjugation endings for each conjugation (-āre, -ēre, -ĕre, -īre).

- **1st Conjugation (-āre):** amō, amās, amat, amāmus, amātis, amant
- **2nd Conjugation (-ēre):** habeō, habēs, habet, habēmus, habētis, habent
- **3rd Conjugation (-ĕre):** dūcō, dūcis, dūcit, dūcimus, dūcitis, dūcunt
- **4th Conjugation (-īre):** audiō, audīs, audit, audīmus, audītis, audiunt

Imperfect Tense - (Tempus Imperfectum)

The imperfect tense is used to describe past habitual actions, ongoing actions in the past, or to set a scene in the past.

Example:

- **Ego edēbam.** - (I was eating / I used to eat.)

How to create: Add the imperfect endings (-bam, -bās, -bat, -bāmus, -bātis, -bant) to the present stem.

Example:

- edĕre → ego edēbam

Key Changes: Learn the imperfect endings for each conjugation.

- **1st Conjugation:** amābam, amābās, amābat, amābāmus, amābātis, amābant
- **2nd Conjugation:** habēbam, habēbās, habēbat, habēbāmus, habēbātis, habēbant

- 3rd Conjugation: dūcēbam, dūcēbās, dūcēbat, dūcēbāmus, dūcēbātis, dūcēbant
- 4th Conjugation: audiēbam, audiēbās, audiēbat, audiēbāmus, audiēbātis, audiēbant

Perfect Tense - (Tempus Perfectum)

The perfect tense is used to describe completed actions in the past.

Example:

- **Ego edī.** - (I ate.)

How to create: Add the perfect endings (-ī, -istī, -it, -imus, -istis, -ērunt) to the perfect stem.

Example:

- edĕre ➔ ego edī

Key Changes: Learn the perfect endings for each conjugation.

- 1st Conjugation: amāvī, amāvistī, amāvit, amāvimus, amāvistis, amāvērunt
- 2nd Conjugation: habuī, habuistī, habuit, habuimus, habuistis, habuērunt
- 3rd Conjugation: dūxī, dūxistī, dūxit, dūximus, dūxistis, dūxērunt
- 4th Conjugation: audīvī, audīvistī, audīvit, audīvimus, audīvistis, audīvērunt

Future Tense - (Tempus Futurum)

The future tense is used to describe actions that will happen in the future.

Example:

- **Ego edam.** - (I will eat.)

How to create: Add the future endings to the present stem. For the 1st and 2nd conjugations, use (-bō, -bis, -bit, -bimus, -bitis, -bunt). For the 3rd and 4th conjugations, use (-am, -ēs, -et, -ēmus, -ētis, -ent).

Example:

- edĕre ➔ ego edam

Key Changes: Learn the future endings for each conjugation.

- 1st Conjugation: amābō, amābis, amābit, amābimus, amābitis, amābunt
- 2nd Conjugation: habēbō, habēbis, habēbit, habēbimus, habēbitis, habēbunt
- 3rd Conjugation: dūcam, dūcēs, dūcet, dūcēmus, dūcētis, dūcent

- 4th Conjugation: audiam, audiēs, audiet, audiēmus, audiētis, audient

Pluperfect Tense - (Tempus Plusquamperfectum)

The pluperfect tense is used to describe actions that had happened before another action in the past.

Example:

- **Ego edĕram.** - (I had eaten.)

How to create: Add the pluperfect endings (-eram, -erās, -erat, -erāmus, -erātis, -erant) to the perfect stem.

Example:

- edĕre → ego edĕram

Key Changes: Learn the pluperfect endings for each conjugation.

- 1st Conjugation: amāveram, amāverās, amāverat, amāverāmus, amāverātis, amāverant
- 2nd Conjugation: habueram, habuerās, habuerat, habuerāmus, habuerātis, habuerant
- 3rd Conjugation: dūxeram, dūxerās, dūxerat, dūxerāmus, dūxerātis, dūxerant
- 4th Conjugation: audīveram, audīverās, audīverat, audīverāmus, audīverātis, audīverant

Future Perfect Tense - (Tempus Futurum Exactum)

The future perfect tense is used to describe actions that will have happened before another future action.

Example:

- **Ego ederō.** - (I will have eaten.)

How to create: Add the future perfect endings (-erō, -eris, -erit, -erimus, -eritis, -erint) to the perfect stem.

Example:

- edĕre → ego ederō

Key Changes: Learn the future perfect endings for each conjugation.

- 1st Conjugation: amāverō, amāveris, amāverit, amāverimus, amāveritis, amāverint
- 2nd Conjugation: habuero, habueris, habuerit, habuerimus, habueritis, habuerint
- 3rd Conjugation: dūxerō, dūxeris, dūxerit, dūxerimus, dūxeritis, dūxerint
- 4th Conjugation: audīverō, audīveris, audīverit, audīverimus, audīveritis, audīverint

Summary of Key Tenses in Latin:

- **Present Tense (Tempus Praesens):** Describes actions currently happening, habitual actions, or general truths.
- **Imperfect Tense (Tempus Imperfectum):** Describes past habitual actions, ongoing actions in the past, or sets a scene in the past.
- **Perfect Tense (Tempus Perfectum):** Describes completed actions in the past.
- **Future Tense (Tempus Futurum):** Describes actions that will happen in the future.
- **Pluperfect Tense (Tempus Plusquamperfectum):** Describes actions that had happened before another action in the past.
- **Future Perfect Tense (Tempus Futurum Exactum):** Describes actions that will have happened before another future action.

Understanding and mastering these tenses is essential for reading, writing, and speaking Latin fluently.

Infinitive	Perfect Stem	Present Tense (Ego)	Imperfect Tense (Ego)	Perfect Tense (Ego)	Future Tense (Ego)	Pluperfect Tense (Ego)	Future Perfect Tense (Ego)
amāre (to love)	amāv-	amō	amābam	amāvī	amābō	amāveram	amāverō
vidēre (to see)	vīd-	videō	vidēbam	vīdī	vidēbō	vīderam	vīderō
dūcere (to lead)	dūx-	dūcō	dūcēbam	dūxī	dūcam	dūxeram	dūxerō

audīre (to hear)	audīv-	audiō	audiēbam	audīvī	audiam	audīveram	audīverō
capere (to take)	cēp-	capiō	capiēbam	cēpī	capiam	cēperam	cēperō

Perfect Passive Participle Examples:

Verb	Perfect Passive Participle	Example
esse (to be)	**fuit** (been)	**Fuit** (I have been)
habēre (to have)	**habitum** (had)	**Habui** (I have had)
facere (to do/make)	**factum** (done/made)	**Feci** (I have done/made)
dicere (to say)	**dictum** (said)	**Dixi** (I have said)
vidēre (to see)	**visum** (seen)	**Vidi** (I have seen)
capere (to take)	**captum** (taken)	**Cepi** (I have taken)
ponere (to put)	**positum** (put)	**Posui** (I have put)
scribere (to write)	**scriptum** (written)	**Scripsi** (I have written)

legere (to read)	**lectum** (read)	**Legi** (I have read)
posse (to be able to)	**potui** (been able to)	**Potui** (I have been able to)
velle (to want)	**volui** (wanted)	**Volui** (I have wanted)
debēre (to owe/must)	**debitum** (had to)	**Debui** (I have had to)
scīre (to know)	**scitum** (known)	**Scivi** (I have known)
bibere (to drink)	**bibitum** (drunk)	**Bibi** (I have drunk)
venīre (to come)	**ventum** (come)	**Veni** (I have come)
vivere (to live)	**victum** (lived)	**Vixi** (I have lived)
aperīre (to open)	**apertum** (opened)	**Aperui** (I have opened)
currere (to run)	**cursum** (run)	**Cucurri** (I have run)
tenēre (to hold)	**tentum** (held)	**Tenui** (I have held)
cognoscere (to know)	**cognitum** (known)	**Cognovi** (I have known)

discere (to learn)	**doctum** (learned)	**Didici** (I have learned)
comprehendere (to understand)	**comprehensum** (understood)	**Comprehendi** (I have understood)
offere (to offer)	**oblatum** (offered)	**Obtuli** (I have offered)
patī (to suffer)	**passum** (suffered)	**Passus sum** (I have suffered)
ridēre (to laugh)	**risum** (laughed)	**Risi** (I have laughed)
sequī (to follow)	**secutum** (followed)	**Secutus sum** (I have followed)
mori (to die)	**mortuum** (died)	**Mortuus sum** (I have died)
nasci (to be born)	**natum** (born)	**Natus sum** (I was born)
recipere (to receive)	**receptum** (received)	**Recepi** (I have received)

These Latin examples reflect the perfect tense construction, which expresses a completed action, equivalent to "I have [done something]" in English. The perfect passive participle is often used with "sum" or "fui" (depending on the context) to convey the past perfect or completed action.

3.3 Word Order in Latin

Latin is often celebrated for its flexibility in word order, a characteristic that sets it apart from many modern languages. Unlike English, which relies heavily on a fixed word order to convey meaning, Latin allows for a wide variety of word arrangements due to its inflected nature. In Latin, the endings of words (inflections) indicate their grammatical function in a sentence, allowing for a more fluid placement of words without losing clarity.

However, despite this flexibility, Latin does have some conventions and tendencies in its word order that can help students grasp the subtleties of the language.

The Basic Structure: Subject-Object-Verb (SOV)

The most common word order in Latin, especially in classical texts, is Subject-Object-Verb (SOV). This structure places the subject of the sentence first, followed by the object, and finally the verb.

Example:

- *Puella librum legit.*
  (The girl reads the book.)

In this sentence, *puella* (girl) is the subject, *librum* (book) is the object, and *legit* (reads) is the verb. The SOV structure is the default order, often used in neutral or straightforward sentences.

Variations in Word Order

While SOV is the default word order, Latin frequently deviates from this pattern for various reasons, including emphasis, style, and poetic meter. Here are some common variations:

1. **Subject-Verb-Object (SVO):**
   This order is similar to English and is often used when the focus is on the action rather than the object.
   Example:
   - *Puella legit librum.*
     (The girl reads the book.)
2. Here, the emphasis is slightly shifted to the action of reading.
3. **Verb-Subject-Object (VSO):**
   This order can be used to emphasize the verb or action.
   Example:
   - *Legit puella librum.*
     (Reads the girl the book.)
4. In this arrangement, *legit* (reads) is emphasized, highlighting the action over the subject or object.
5. **Object-Subject-Verb (OSV):**
   This structure emphasizes the object of the sentence.
   Example:
   - *Librum puella legit.*
     (The book, the girl reads.)
6. By placing *librum* (book) at the beginning, the sentence draws attention to what is being read.

7. **Object-Verb-Subject (OVS):**
   This order is used to highlight the object while keeping the verb close to it, often for stylistic reasons.
   Example:
   - *Librum legit puella.*
     (The book is read by the girl.)
8. The focus here is on the object and the action, with the subject appearing at the end.

Emphasis and Rhetorical Effect

Latin word order is not just about grammar; it's also a tool for emphasis and rhetorical effect. By rearranging words, Latin speakers and writers could draw attention to specific elements of a sentence, change the tone, or create a particular mood. For example:

- **Emphasizing the Subject:** Placing the subject at the beginning or end of a sentence can draw attention to it.
  Example:
  - *Legit librum puella.*
    (It is the girl who reads the book.)
- The focus is on the girl as the one performing the action.
- **Emphasizing the Object:** Placing the object at the beginning of the sentence can emphasize its importance or the action being done to it.
  Example:
  - *Librum puella legit.*
    (The book is what the girl reads.)
- The book is highlighted as the key element of the sentence.
- **Emphasizing the Verb:** Placing the verb at the beginning or end of a sentence can highlight the action itself.
  Example:
  - *Legit librum puella.*
    (Reading is what the girl does.)
- The action of reading is brought to the forefront.

Adjectives and Nouns

Adjectives in Latin typically follow the nouns they modify, but this is not a strict rule. The placement of adjectives can vary depending on the desired emphasis.

Example:

- *Puella pulchra* (The beautiful girl)
- *Pulchra puella* (The beautiful girl)

In the first example, the emphasis is on the girl, while in the second, the emphasis shifts slightly to her beauty. In poetry and more stylized prose, adjectives might be placed far from the noun they modify, creating a pleasing or dramatic effect.

Prepositions and Their Objects

Prepositions in Latin usually precede their objects, much like in English. However, in poetry or for emphasis, the preposition can sometimes follow its object, creating a more artistic or impactful sentence.

Example:

- *In urbe* (In the city)
- *Urbe in* (In the city - with emphasis or poetic effect)

This inversion is more common in Latin poetry and is used to maintain meter or to create a specific rhythm.

The Role of Enclitics

Enclitics are short words that attach themselves to the end of a preceding word. In Latin, enclitics like *-que* (and) or *-ne* (a question marker) can influence word order by requiring their host word to appear in a specific position within the sentence.

Example:

- *Puella puerque veniunt.*
  (The girl and boy are coming.)
- *Venitne puella?*
  (Is the girl coming?)

The enclitic *-que* is added to *puer* (boy) to connect it with *puella* (girl), and *-ne* attaches to the verb to form a question.

Conclusion: Mastering Latin Word Order

Understanding Latin word order is a key component of mastering the language. While its flexibility offers a wide range of expressive possibilities, recognizing the patterns and conventions can significantly aid comprehension and fluency. Practice by reading Latin texts, noting how authors use word order to convey emphasis, mood, and style, will deepen your understanding of this ancient language.

Ultimately, the ability to manipulate word order not only allows for more nuanced communication but also provides insight into the literary and rhetorical techniques employed by Roman writers, poets, and orators.

3.4 Cases in Latin Grammar

In Latin, the concept of grammatical cases is fundamental to understanding sentence structure. Unlike Spanish, where word order plays a more significant role, Latin relies on word endings to indicate the role of each noun in a sentence. Latin has six primary cases, each serving a distinct purpose. These cases include the nominative, accusative, genitive, dative, ablative, and vocative. Each case answers specific questions about the noun's role in the sentence, such as who is doing the action, to whom the action is done, or in what manner something is done.

1. Nominative Case

The **nominative case** is used for the subject of the sentence, the one performing the action.

- **Question:** Who or what is doing the action?
- **Example:**
    - *Puella legit.* - The girl reads.

2. Accusative Case

The **accusative case** is used for the direct object of the verb, the one directly receiving the action.

- **Question:** Who or what is directly affected by the action?
- **Example:**
    - *Puella librum legit.* - The girl reads the book.

3. Genitive Case

The **genitive case** indicates possession, similar to the English possessive "of" or the possessive apostrophe 's.

- **Question:** Whose? Of what?
- **Example:**
    - *Liber puellae est.* - The book is the girl's (The book of the girl).

4. Dative Case

The **dative case** is used for the indirect object, showing to whom or for whom the action is done.

- **Question:** To whom? For whom?
- **Example:**
    - *Puella amico librum dat.* - The girl gives the book to the friend.

5. Ablative Case

The **ablative case** has several functions, often used to indicate means or instrument (by/with what), cause, manner, or sometimes separation or place where.

- **Questions:** By what means? With what? From where? In what manner?
- **Example:**
    - *Puella cum amico ambulat.* - The girl walks with the friend.
    - *Puella in urbe habitat.* - The girl lives in the city.

6. Vocative Case

The **vocative case** is used for direct address, calling someone by name or title.

- **Question:** O (person)?
- **Example:**
    - *Salve, amice!* - Hello, friend!

Understanding Case Endings

In Latin, nouns are grouped into five declensions, each with its own set of endings for the different cases. Below is a simplified overview of the case endings for the first and second declensions, which are among the most common in Latin:

Case	1st Declension (feminine)	2nd Declension (masculine)	2nd Declension (neuter)
Nominative	-a (puella)	-us (servus) / -er (puer)	-um (bellum)
Accusative	-am (puellam)	-um (servum)	-um (bellum)
Genitive	-ae (puellae)	-i (servi)	-i (belli)
Dative	-ae (puellae)	-o (servo)	-o (bello)
Ablative	-a (puella)	-o (servo)	-o (bello)
Vocative	-a (puella)	-e (serve) / -er (puer)	-um (bellum)

Example Sentences Using All Cases

1. **Nominative Case:** *Puella ridet.* - The girl laughs.
2. **Accusative Case:** *Puella puerum videt.* - The girl sees the boy.
3. **Genitive Case:** *Liber pueri est.* - The book is the boy's.
4. **Dative Case:** *Puella amico librum dat.* - The girl gives the book to the friend.
5. **Ablative Case:** *Puella cum puero ambulat.* - The girl walks with the boy.
6. **Vocative Case:** *O puella, veni!* - O girl, come!

Importance of Word Order

While Latin has a flexible word order due to its use of cases, understanding the basic structure and common patterns will help you comprehend and construct Latin sentences effectively. For example, placing the subject in the nominative case first, followed by the object in the accusative case, and then the verb (SOV structure) is a common pattern, though variations are used for emphasis or style.

3.5 Perfect Tense in Latin Grammar

The Perfect Tense in Latin is used to describe actions that have been completed in the past. It is one of the key tenses in Latin for expressing past actions, and it corresponds closely to the English simple past ("I loved") or present perfect ("I have loved").

Formation of the Perfect Tense

The Perfect Tense is formed by adding specific endings to the perfect stem of the verb. The perfect stem is found by removing the "-i" from the first person singular form of the verb in the Perfect Active Indicative.

Regular Verbs

Here is how the Perfect Tense is formed for regular verbs in each conjugation:

- **1st Conjugation (-are verbs): Perfect Stem** = Remove "-i" from the first person singular form in the Perfect Indicative.
  - Example: *amo* (I love) → *amavi* (I loved)
  - **Endings:**
    - **Ego (I):** -i → *amavi* (I loved)
    - **Tu (you):** -isti → *amavisti* (you loved)
    - **Is/Ea/Id (he/she/it):** -it → *amavit* (he/she/it loved)
    - **Nos (we):** -imus → *amavimus* (we loved)
    - **Vos (you all):** -istis → *amavistis* (you all loved)
    - **Ei/Eae/Ea (they):** -erunt/-ere → *amaverunt/amavere* (they loved)

- **2nd Conjugation** (-ēre verbs):
    - Example: *moneo* (I warn) → *monui* (I warned)
    - **Endings:**
        - **Ego:** -i → monui (I warned)
        - **Tu:** -isti → monuisti (you warned)
        - **Is/Ea/Id:** -it → monuit (he/she/it warned)
        - **Nos:** -imus → monuimus (we warned)
        - **Vos:** -istis → monuistis (you all warned)
        - **Ei/Eae/Ea:** -erunt/-ere → monuerunt/monuere (they warned)
- **3rd Conjugation** (-ere verbs):
    - Example: *rego* (I rule) → *rexi* (I ruled)
    - **Endings:**
        - **Ego:** -i → rexi (I ruled)
        - **Tu:** -isti → rexisti (you ruled)
        - **Is/Ea/Id:** -it → rexit (he/she/it ruled)
        - **Nos:** -imus → reximus (we ruled)
        - **Vos:** -istis → rexistis (you all ruled)
        - **Ei/Eae/Ea:** -erunt/-ere → rexerunt/rexere (they ruled)
- **4th Conjugation** (-ire verbs):
    - Example: *audio* (I hear) → *audivi* (I heard)
    - **Endings:**
        - **Ego:** -i → audivi (I heard)
        - **Tu:** -isti → audivisti (you heard)
        - **Is/Ea/Id:** -it → audivit (he/she/it heard)
        - **Nos:** -imus → audivimus (we heard)
        - **Vos:** -istis → audivistis (you all heard)
        - **Ei/Eae/Ea:** -erunt/-ere → audiverunt/audivere (they heard)

Irregular Verbs

Some verbs in Latin are irregular and have unique stems in the Perfect Tense. Below are a few common irregular verbs:

- **Sum (to be):**
    - Ego fui - I was
    - Tu fuisti - You were
    - Is/Ea/Id fuit - He/She/It was
    - Nos fuimus - We were
    - Vos fuistis - You all were
    - Ei/Eae/Ea fuerunt - They were

- **Eo (to go):**
    - Ego ii/ivi - I went
    - Tu isti/ivisti - You went
    - Is/Ea/Id iit/ivit - He/She/It went
    - Nos iimus/ivimus - We went
    - Vos istis/ivistis - You all went
    - Ei/Eae/Ea ierunt/iverunt - They went
- **Volo (to want):**
    - Ego volui - I wanted
    - Tu voluisti - You wanted
    - Is/Ea/Id voluit - He/She/It wanted
    - Nos voluimus - We wanted
    - Vos voluistis - You all wanted
    - Ei/Eae/Ea voluerunt - They wanted

Usage of the Perfect Tense

The Perfect Tense in Latin is used to describe actions that were completed in the past. It is a vital tense for expressing past actions and is often used in narratives, historical writings, and legal texts.

Examples

- **Narrative:**
    - *Caesar Galliam vicit.* - Caesar conquered Gaul.
- **Historical Writing:**
    - *Romani Carthaginem deleverunt.* - The Romans destroyed Carthage.
- **Legal Text:**
    - *Senatus consultum fecit.* - The Senate passed a decree.

Understanding the Perfect Tense in Latin is essential for interpreting and constructing sentences about past events.

3.6 Infinitive with "Ad" in Latin

In Latin, certain verbs are followed by the preposition "ad" before an infinitive verb. This construction often indicates purpose or direction of an action. Understanding which verbs require "ad" is essential for constructing grammatically correct and meaningful sentences in Latin.

Here are some frequently used Latin verbs that are typically followed by "ad" when they are followed by an infinitive:

1. **Auxiliari ad** - *to help to*
   - **Example:** *Me adiuvas ad studendum.* - You help me to study.
2. **Discere ad** - *to learn to*
   - **Example:** *Disco ad coquendum.* - I am learning to cook.
3. **Incipere ad** - *to begin to*
   - **Example:** *Incipimus ad laborandum mane.* - We begin to work early.
4. **Instruere ad** - *to teach to*
   - **Example:** *Me instruxit ad natandum.* - He/She taught me to swim.
5. **Invitare ad** - *to invite to*
   - **Example:** *Nos invitavit ad cenandum.* - They invited us to dinner.
6. **Ire ad** - *to go to*
   - **Example:** *Vado ad studendum nunc.* - I am going to study now.
7. **Redire ad** - *to do something again*
   - **Example:** *Iterum redeo ad temptandum.* - I return to try again.
8. **Assuefacere ad** - *to get used to*
   - **Example:** *Assuefacio ad vivendum hic.* - I am getting used to living here.
9. **Recusare ad** - *to refuse to*
   - **Example:** *Recusavit ad adiuvandum.* - He/She refused to help.

Examples:

1. **Incipio ad scribendum.** - *I begin to write.*
2. **Disci ad Latine loquendum.** - *I learn to speak Latin.*
3. **Vado ad ludendum.** - *I am going to play now.*
4. **Invitat nos ad convivium.** - *He/She invites us to the banquet.*
5. **Assuefacimur ad surgendum mane.** - *We are getting used to waking up early.*

Special Cases and Nuances

- **Verbs with a Change in Meaning:** Some verbs change their meaning when used with "ad" + infinitive.
    - **Incipere ad** - *to begin to*
        - **Example:** *Incipio ad studendum.* - *I begin to study.*
- **Idiomatic Expressions:** Some verbs and expressions are idiomatic and must be learned as fixed phrases.
    - **Ponere ad + infinitive** - *to start doing something*
        - **Example:** *Ponitur ad laborandum statim.* - *He/She starts working right away.*
    - **Ire ad + infinitive** - *to be going to (do something)*
        - **Example:** *Vado ad studendum.* - *I am going to study.*

3.7 Reflexive Verbs in Latin

In Latin, reflexive verbs are verbs where the action reflects back on the subject. These verbs are conjugated with reflexive pronouns that correspond to the subject of the sentence. Reflexive verbs are common in Latin and are used to indicate actions that the subject performs on themselves.

Reflexive pronouns in Latin are:

- **me** (myself)
- **te** (yourself, informal)
- **se** (himself, herself, itself, themselves)
- **nos** (ourselves)
- **vos** (yourselves, informal plural)

These pronouns are typically used in the accusative or ablative case, depending on the verb and its construction.

To conjugate a reflexive verb in Latin, place the correct reflexive pronoun in the sentence, often following the verb, and conjugate the verb according to the subject and tense. Reflexive verbs in Latin often follow the same conjugation patterns as their non-reflexive counterparts, with the reflexive pronoun indicating that the subject is both performing and receiving the action.

Example: Lavare (to wash oneself)

Present Tense:

- *Ego* **me lavo** (I wash myself)
- *Tu* **te lavas** (You wash yourself)
- *Is/Ea/Id* **se lavat** (He/She/It washes himself/herself/itself)
- *Nos* **nos lavamus** (We wash ourselves)
- *Vos* **vos lavatis** (You all wash yourselves)
- *Ei/Eae/Ea* **se lavant** (They wash themselves)

Imperfect Tense:

- *Ego* **me lavabam** (I was washing myself)
- *Tu* **te lavabas** (You were washing yourself)
- *Is/Ea/Id* **se lavabat** (He/She/It was washing himself/herself/itself)
- *Nos* **nos lavabamus** (We were washing ourselves)
- *Vos* **vos lavabatis** (You all were washing yourselves)
- *Ei/Eae/Ea* **se lavabant** (They were washing themselves)

Here are some commonly used reflexive verbs in Latin:

- **Despergere (to wake up oneself)**
  - *Me despergo hora septima.* (I wake up at 7.)
- **Surgere (to get up oneself)**
  - *Te surgis mane.* (You get up early.)
- **Cubitum ire (to go to bed)**
  - *Nos cubitum imus sero.* (We go to bed late.)
- **Vestire (to get dressed oneself)**
  - *Se vestit celeriter.* (He/She gets dressed quickly.)
- **Dentem purgare (to brush one's teeth)**
  - *Me dentes purgo.* (I brush my teeth.)
- **Radere (to shave oneself)**
  - *Se radit omni mane.* (He/She shaves every morning.)
- **Pectere (to comb one's hair)**
  - *Me pecto ante speculum.* (I comb my hair in front of the mirror.)
- **Ornare (to adorn oneself, to put on makeup)**
  - *Se ornat antequam exit.* (She puts on makeup before going out.)
- **Quiescere (to rest oneself)**
  - *Nos quiescimus post laborem.* (We rest after work.)
- **Festinare (to hurry oneself)**
  - *Se festinant ne sero veniant.* (They hurry so as not to be late.)

Special Cases and Nuances

- **Idiomatic Expressions:** Some reflexive verbs in Latin are idiomatic, meaning their meaning cannot be deduced from the individual words.
  - **Abire (to go away)**
    - *Me abeo.* (I'm leaving.)
- **Reflexive Verbs in Different Tenses:** Reflexive verbs follow the same conjugation rules as non-reflexive verbs in different tenses. Just remember to include the correct reflexive pronoun.
  Future:
  - *Me cubitum ibo hac nocte.* (I'm going to bed early tonight.)
- **Commands:** In the imperative, reflexive pronouns come after the verb. Latin typically omits the subject pronoun in imperatives.
  Affirmative:
  - **Surge!** (Get up!)
- **Negative:**
  - **Noli surgere!** (Don't get up!)

Understanding reflexive verbs in Latin is essential for constructing sentences where the action of the verb directly affects the subject.

3.8 Transitive and Intransitive Verbs in Latin

In Latin, verbs are also categorized as transitive or intransitive, based on whether they require a direct object to complete their meaning. Understanding the distinction between these types of verbs is crucial for constructing correct Latin sentences.

Transitive Verbs

Transitive verbs (verba transitiva) require a direct object to complete their meaning. The action of the verb is transferred directly to the object, typically in the accusative case.

Examples:

- **Videre** (to see)
    - *Vir librum videt.* - The man sees the book.
    - *(Vir LEE-brum WI-det.)*
- **Amare** (to love)
    - *Femina puerum amat.* - The woman loves the boy.
    - *(FEM-ee-nah PWEH-rum AH-mat.)*
- **Legere** (to read)
    - *Discipulus epistulam legit.* - The student reads the letter.
    - *(Dis-KIP-uh-lus eh-PIS-too-lahm LEH-git.)*
- **Scribere** (to write)
    - *Poeta carmen scribit.* - The poet writes a poem.
    - *(POH-eh-tah KAR-men SKREE-bit.)*
- **Tangere** (to touch)
    - *Puella florem tangit.* - The girl touches the flower.
    - *(PWEH-lah FLOR-em TAN-git.)*

Intransitive Verbs

Intransitive verbs (verba intransitiva) do not require a direct object. The action of the verb does not transfer to an object but rather stays with the subject.

Examples:

- **Dormire** (to sleep)
    - *Puella bene dormit.* - The girl sleeps well.
    - *(PWEH-lah BEH-neh DOR-mit.)*
- **Venire** (to come)
    - *Milites veniunt.* - The soldiers come.

- o *(MIH-lee-tehs WEH-nee-oont.)*
- **Morari** (to delay)
  - o *Imperator moratur.* - The commander delays.
  - o *(Im-peh-RAH-tor mo-RAH-tur.)*
- **Surgere** (to rise)
  - o *Sol surgit.* - The sun rises.
  - o *(SOL SOOR-git.)*
- **Currere** (to run)
  - o *Equi currunt.* - The horses run.
  - o *(EH-kwee KOOR-runt.)*

Verbs That Can Be Both Transitive and Intransitive

Some verbs can function as both transitive and intransitive, depending on how they are used in a sentence.

Examples:

- **Movere** (to move)
  - o **Transitive:** *Agricola plaustrum movet.* - The farmer moves the cart.
  - o *(Ah-GREE-koh-lah PLAUS-trum MOH-wet.)*
  - o **Intransitive:** *Stellae movent.* - The stars move.
  - o *(STEL-lah-ee MOH-went.)*
- **Caedere** (to cut)
  - o **Transitive:** *Lignator arborem caedit.* - The woodcutter cuts the tree.
  - o *(Lig-NAH-tor AR-boh-rem KAI-dit.)*
  - o **Intransitive:** *Gladius caedit.* - The sword cuts.
  - o *(GLAH-dee-us KAI-dit.)*
- **Manere** (to stay, to remain)
  - o **Transitive:** *Milites castra manent.* - The soldiers stay in the camp.
  - o *(MIH-lee-tehs KAS-trah MAH-nent.)*
  - o **Intransitive:** *Nocte manent.* - They remain during the night.
  - o *(NOK-teh MAH-nent.)*
- **Facere** (to make, to do)
  - o **Transitive:** *Rex templum facit.* - The king builds a temple.
  - o *(Reks TEM-plum FAH-kit.)*
  - o **Intransitive:** *Sol facit.* - The sun acts/moves.
  - o *(SOL FAH-kit.)*
- **Crescere** (to grow)
  - o **Transitive:** *Agricola frumentum crescit.* - The farmer grows wheat.
  - o *(Ah-GREE-koh-lah froo-MEN-toom KREH-skit.)*

- Intransitive: *Flos crescit.* - The flower grows.
- (Flos KREH-skit.)

Identifying Transitive and Intransitive Verbs

To identify whether a verb is transitive or intransitive in Latin, consider the following:

- **Does the verb need a direct object to make sense?**
    - If yes, it is transitive.
    - If no, it is intransitive.
- **Can the verb be followed directly by a noun in the accusative case without a preposition?**
    - If yes, it is transitive.
    - If no, it is intransitive.

Examples:

- **Transitive:**
    - *Feminam amo.* - I love the woman.
    - (FEM-ee-nahm AH-mo.)
- **Intransitive:**
    - *Bene dormio.* - I sleep well.
    - (BEH-neh DOR-mee-o.)

Understanding whether a verb is transitive or intransitive is key to using Latin verbs correctly and constructing grammatically accurate sentences.

3.9 The Passive Voice in Latin

In Latin, the passive voice is used similarly to other languages to emphasize the action or the recipient of the action rather than the doer (agent). It is an essential aspect of Latin grammar, particularly in historical, literary, and formal texts.

Forming the Passive Voice

To form the passive voice in Latin, the verb is conjugated in the passive form. The passive endings differ depending on the verb conjugation and tense. Latin does not always explicitly state the agent performing the action; when the agent is mentioned, it is typically introduced by the preposition "ā/ab" (by).

Structure:

- **Subject + Passive Verb Form + (ā/ab + Agent)**

Examples in Different Tenses

Present Tense:

- **Active:** *Magister discipulos docet.*
  (The teacher teaches the students.)
  (Mah-GIS-ter dis-kee-poo-los DOH-ket.)
- **Passive:** *Discipuli a magistro docentur.*
  (The students are taught by the teacher.)
  (Dis-kee-poo-lee ah Mah-GIS-tro doh-KEN-toor.)

Imperfect Tense:

- **Active:** *Puella librum legebat.*
  (The girl was reading the book.)
  (PWEH-lah LEE-brum LEH-ge-bat.)
- **Passive:** *Liber a puella legebatur.*
  (The book was being read by the girl.)
  (LEE-ber ah PWEH-lah leh-geh-BAH-toor.)

Future Tense:

- **Active:** *Milites castra aedificabunt.*
  (The soldiers will build the camp.)
  (MIH-lee-tehs KAS-trah aeh-di-fi-KAH-boont.)
- **Passive:** *Castra a militibus aedificabuntur.*
  (The camp will be built by the soldiers.)
  (KAS-trah ah MIH-lee-tee-boos aeh-di-fi-KAH-boon-toor.)

Perfect Tense:

- **Active:** *Romani urbem ceperunt.*
  (The Romans captured the city.)
  (Roh-MAH-nee OOR-bem keh-PEH-roont.)
- **Passive:** *Urbs a Romanis capta est.*
  (The city was captured by the Romans.)
  (OORBS ah Roh-MAH-nees KAP-tah est.)

Pluperfect Tense:

- **Active:** *Hostes muros deleverant.*
  (The enemies had destroyed the walls.)
  (HOS-tehs MOO-ros deh-LEH-weh-rant.)
- **Passive:** *Muri a hostibus deleti erant.*
  (The walls had been destroyed by the enemies.)
  (MOO-ree ah HOS-ti-boos deh-LEE-tee eh-rant.)

Passive Voice Endings

The passive voice endings in Latin vary according to the verb conjugation and tense. Here are the basic passive endings for the present, imperfect, and future tenses:

- **Present Tense:**
  -or, -ris, -tur, -mur, -mini, -ntur
- **Imperfect Tense:**
  -bar, -baris, -batur, -bamur, -bamini, -bantur
- **Future Tense:**
  -bor, -beris, -bitur, -bimur, -bimini, -buntur (1st and 2nd conjugations)
  -ar, -eris, -etur, -emur, -emini, -entur (3rd and 4th conjugations)

Using "Ā/Ab" with the Agent

In Latin, when the agent (the doer of the action) is expressed, the preposition "ā" (before a consonant) or "ab" (before a vowel or h) is used:

Examples:

- *Urbs ab hostibus capta est.*
  (The city was captured by the enemies.)
  (OORBS ab HOS-ti-boos KAP-tah est.)
- *Liber a Marco scriptus est.*
  (The book was written by Marcus.)
  (LEE-ber ah MAR-koh SKRIP-toos est.)

Agreement of the Past Participle

When forming the perfect, pluperfect, and future perfect passive tenses, the past participle must agree with the subject in gender, number, and case.

Examples:

- **Feminine Singular:**
  Epistula scripta est.
  (The letter was written.)
  (eh-PIS-too-lah SKRIP-tah est.)
- **Masculine Plural:**
  Viri laudati sunt.
  (The men were praised.)
  (WEE-ree lau-DAH-tee soont.)

Understanding the Passive Voice

Mastering the passive voice in Latin enables you to read and translate texts where the focus is on the action or its recipient rather than the doer. This voice is frequently used in formal writing, historical accounts, and literature.

Conjugation of Deponent Verbs

Deponent verbs in Latin are a unique category of verbs that, while passive in form, convey an active meaning. These verbs do not have active forms, and their conjugation patterns align with passive verbs, even though their meaning is active.

Key Characteristics:

- **Passive Form, Active Meaning:** Deponent verbs are conjugated using passive endings, but their translation is in the active voice.
- **No Active Forms:** Unlike other Latin verbs, deponent verbs lack active forms in all tenses.
- **Three Conjugations:** Deponent verbs can belong to any of the three conjugations, and they follow the passive conjugation patterns of their respective conjugation group.

Common Deponent Verbs:

- *loquor, loqui, locutus sum* – to speak
- *sequor, sequi, secutus sum* – to follow
- *morior, mori, mortuus sum* – to die
- *orior, oriri, ortus sum* – to rise

Example of Conjugation:

Let's consider the verb *loquor* (to speak):

Present Indicative:

- loquor (I speak)

- loqueris (you speak)
- loquitur (he/she/it speaks)
- loquimur (we speak)
- loquimini (you all speak)
- loquuntur (they speak)

Imperfect Indicative:

- loquebar (I was speaking)
- loquebaris (you were speaking)
- loquebatur (he/she/it was speaking)
- loquebamur (we were speaking)
- loquebamini (you all were speaking)
- loquebantur (they were speaking)

Future Indicative:

- loquar (I will speak)
- loqueris (you will speak)
- loquetur (he/she/it will speak)
- loquemur (we will speak)
- loquemini (you all will speak)
- loquentur (they will speak)

Deponent verbs are essential in Latin literature, often appearing in philosophical and historical texts. Understanding their conjugation allows you to accurately interpret sentences where the passive form might initially confuse a reader unfamiliar with deponents.

Irregular Verbs

Irregular verbs in Latin are those that do not follow the regular conjugation patterns of their respective groups. These verbs are fundamental and frequently used in both classical and medieval Latin texts.

Key Irregular Verbs:

1. **Sum, esse, fui, futurus** – to be
2. **Possum, posse, potui** – to be able
3. **Volo, velle, volui** – to want
4. **Nolo, nolle, nolui** – to not want
5. **Fero, ferre, tuli, latus** – to bring, carry

Conjugation Patterns:

Sum, esse, fui, futurus:

- **Present:** sum, es, est, sumus, estis, sunt
- **Imperfect:** eram, eras, erat, eramus, eratis, erant
- **Future:** ero, eris, erit, erimus, eritis, erunt

Possum, posse, potui:

- **Present:** possum, potes, potest, possumus, potestis, possunt
- **Imperfect:** poteram, poteras, poterat, poteramus, poteratis, poterant
- **Future:** potero, poteris, poterit, poterimus, poteritis, poterunt

Volo, velle, volui:

- **Present:** volo, vis, vult, volumus, vultis, volunt
- **Imperfect:** volebam, volebas, volebat, volebamus, volebatis, volebant
- **Future:** volam, voles, volet, volemus, voletis, volent

Understanding these irregular verbs is crucial as they appear frequently across all types of Latin literature, from poetry to legal documents. Their irregular forms must be memorized, as they do not follow standard conjugation rules.

Gerunds and Gerundives

The gerund and gerundive in Latin are verbal nouns and adjectives, respectively, that express necessity, purpose, or obligation. They are unique in that they blend verbal and nominal aspects, and they are used in various grammatical constructions.

The Gerund:

The gerund is a verbal noun that expresses the action of the verb in an abstract sense. It is declined in the genitive, dative, accusative, and ablative cases, and it is always singular. The nominative case does not exist for gerunds.

Examples:

- **Genitive:** *ars vivendi* (the art of living)
- **Dative:** *paratus ad scribendum* (prepared for writing)
- **Accusative:** *ad dicendum* (for speaking)
- **Ablative:** *in scribendo* (in writing)

The Gerundive:

The gerundive is a verbal adjective that expresses necessity or obligation. It agrees in gender, number, and case with the noun it modifies. It is often used with the verb *esse* to form the passive periphrastic construction, which conveys a sense of duty or necessity.

Examples:

- **Nominative:** *liber legendus est* (the book must be read)
- **Genitive:** *causa vivendi* (the reason for living)
- **Dative:** *librum legendum* (a book to be read)
- **Ablative:** *libro legendum* (by reading a book)

The gerundive is particularly useful in legal and formal texts, where obligations or duties are frequently expressed. Understanding the differences between the gerund and gerundive is essential for interpreting Latin correctly.

Supine

The supine is a verbal noun that appears in two distinct forms in Latin, typically used to express purpose or result. There are two main uses of the supine: the accusative supine and the ablative supine.

Accusative Supine:

The accusative supine is used after verbs of motion to indicate purpose. It is formed by using the fourth principal part of the verb.

Examples:

- *veni dictu* (I came to speak)
- *misit rogatum* (he sent [them] to ask)

Ablative Supine:

The ablative supine is used to express respect or specification, often after adjectives.

Examples:

- *facile dictu* (easy to say)
- *horribile visu* (horrible to see)

The supine is less commonly used than other verbal forms, but it is important in specific literary and legal contexts. Mastery of the supine allows for a deeper understanding of nuanced expressions of purpose in Latin.

Indirect Statements (Oratio Obliqua)

Indirect statements, or *oratio obliqua*, are a common way to report speech or thought in Latin. They are formed by using an accusative subject and an infinitive verb, rather than a conjunction like "that" as in English.

Formation:

- **Main Clause Verb:** A verb of saying, thinking, perceiving, etc.
- **Subject:** Accusative case.
- **Verb:** Infinitive form.

Example:

- **Direct Statement:** *Puella venit* (The girl is coming.)
- **Indirect Statement:** *Dicit puellam venire* (He says that the girl is coming.)

Tense of the Infinitive:

The tense of the infinitive in indirect statements is determined relative to the main verb:

- **Present Infinitive:** Simultaneous action.
- **Perfect Infinitive:** Action prior to the main verb.
- **Future Infinitive:** Action subsequent to the main verb.

Examples:

- *Scio eum venire* (I know that he is coming) – Present Infinitive.
- *Scio eum venisse* (I know that he came) – Perfect Infinitive.
- *Scio eum venturum esse* (I know that he will come) – Future Infinitive.

Indirect statements are prevalent in Latin literature, especially in historical and philosophical texts. They are essential for conveying reported speech and thoughts with precision.

Subjunctive Mood in Subordinate Clauses

The subjunctive mood in Latin is used to express various states of unreality such as doubt, desire, possibility, or necessity. It is commonly used in subordinate clauses introduced by conjunctions.

Purpose Clauses:

Purpose clauses express the intention of an action and are introduced by *ut* (in order that) or *ne* (in order that not).

Examples:

- *Veni ut te videam* (I came in order to see you).
- *Discedit ne capiatur* (He leaves in order not to be captured).

Result Clauses:

Result clauses express the outcome of an action and are introduced by *ut* (so that), often accompanied by adverbs like *tam* (so) or *ita* (thus).

Example:

- *Tam fessus erat ut dormiret* (He was so tired that he slept).

Conditional Clauses:

Conditional clauses, or "if" clauses, often use the subjunctive mood to express hypothetical situations.

Examples:

- *Si venias, laetus sim* (If you should come, I would be happy).
- *Si venisses, laetus fuissem* (If you had come, I would have been happy).

Understanding the use of the subjunctive in these contexts is critical for mastering complex sentence structures in Latin.

Ablative Absolute

The ablative absolute is a grammatical construction that consists of a noun and a participle, both in the ablative case, forming a phrase that is grammatically independent from the main clause.

Formation:

- **Noun:** Ablative case.
- **Participle:** Ablative case.

Examples:

- *Urbe capta, cives fugerunt* (With the city having been captured, the citizens fled).
- *Rege mortuo, res publica restituta est* (With the king having died, the republic was restored).

The ablative absolute is often used to provide background information, setting the scene for the main action of the sentence. It is a concise way to express conditions or circumstances that accompany the main verb.

Impersonal Verbs

Impersonal verbs in Latin do not have a specific subject and are always used in the third person singular. These verbs are often used to express general conditions or actions.

Common Impersonal Verbs:

- **Pluit:** it is raining.
- **Licet:** it is permitted.
- **Necesse est:** it is necessary.

Examples:

- *Pluit hodie* (It is raining today).
- *Necesse est discedere* (It is necessary to leave).

Impersonal verbs are a distinctive feature of Latin, often used to express actions or states of being that do not involve a specific subject.

9. Partitive Genitive

The partitive genitive is used in Latin to express the whole from which a part is taken. It is often used with words indicating quantity or with comparatives.

Formation:

- **Noun in Genitive Case:** The whole.
- **Noun in Nominative or Accusative Case:** The part.

Examples:

- *Pars urbis* (Part of the city).
- *Multum vini* (A lot of wine).

The partitive genitive is common in expressions of quantity and comparison, allowing for precise distinctions between parts and wholes in Latin sentences.

CHAPTER 4: READING PRACTICE

Latin: Lucius, puer rusticus, erat agricolae filius. Lucius in Sicilia, in parva villa rustica cum familia sua, vivebat. Quamquam vitam simplicem agebat, semper somniavit de Roma, urbe magna et plena mirabilium. Unus dies, pater eius dixit, "Lucius, tempus est ut Romam viseres. Tu frumentum ad mercatum magnum portas."

Lucius erat laetus sed paulo timidus. "Roma? Ego? Urbs tam magna?" inquit.

Pater respondit, "Etiam, Luci. Disce de urbe, de hominibus, et de vita in loco diverso. Hoc erit tibi bonum."

Lucius sarcinam paravit et cum frumento iter incipiebat. Via erat longa, sed animus eius plenus erat spe. Omnia nova videbat—maria latissima, montes altissimi, et flumina fluitantia. Post multos dies et noctes, tandem Romam vidit.

English Translation: Lucius, a rustic boy, was the son of a farmer. Lucius lived in Sicily, in a small country house with his family. Although he lived a simple life, he always dreamed of Rome, a great city full of wonders. One day, his father said, "Lucius, it is time for you to visit Rome. You will carry the grain to the great market."

Lucius was happy but a little nervous. "Rome? Me? A city so great?" he said.

His father replied, "Yes, Lucius. Learn about the city, about the people, and about life in a different place. This will be good for you."

Lucius packed his bag and started his journey with the grain. The road was long, but his mind was full of hope. He saw many new things—the vast seas, the tall mountains, and the flowing rivers. After many days and nights, he finally saw Rome.

Latin: Cum Lucius urbem intravit, stupefactus est. Roma erat multo maior quam sibi finxerat. Aedificia alta, templa magna, et turbae hominum ubique erant. Equi currus trahebant per vias, et mercatores clamabant, "Venite, venite! Hic sunt optimae merces!" Lucius numquam antea tantam multitudinem viderat.

Curiosus, Lucius ad forum properavit. Locus plenus erat mercatoribus, oratoribus, et civibus Romanis. Populus Romam veniebat ex omnibus partibus mundi. Lucius, qui solum rusticos et agricolas noverat, se in nova, aliena mundi parte invenit.

English Translation: When Lucius entered the city, he was amazed. Rome was much larger than he had imagined. Tall buildings, great temples, and crowds of people were everywhere. Horses pulled chariots through the streets, and merchants shouted, "Come, come! Here are the best goods!" Lucius had never seen such a crowd before.

Curious, Lucius hurried to the forum. The place was full of merchants, speakers, and Roman citizens. People came to Rome from all parts of the world. Lucius, who had only known rustic people and farmers, found himself in a new, unfamiliar world.

Word List:

- **puer** (boy) - /pweh-r/
- **rusticus** (rustic, country) - /roo-stee-koos/
- **agricolae** (farmer) - /ah-gree-koh-lah-eh/
- **filius** (son) - /fee-lee-oos/
- **villa** (country house) - /vee-lah/
- **vitam** (life) - /vee-tahm/
- **urbem** (city) - /oor-bem/
- **magna** (great) - /mahg-nah/
- **mercatum** (market) - /mehr-kah-toom/
- **sarcinam** (bag) - /sar-kee-nahm/
- **iter** (journey) - /ee-tehr/
- **via** (road) - /wee-ah/
- **Romam** (Rome) - /roh-mahm/
- **aedificia** (buildings) - /ay-dee-fee-see-ah/
- **templa** (temples) - /tem-plah/
- **mercatores** (merchants) - /mehr-kah-toh-rehs/
- **forum** (forum) - /foh-room/
- **populus** (people) - /poh-poo-loos/

Latin: Postquam forum vidit, Lucius audivit de Senatu, magno loco ubi Romani leges fecerunt. Amicus novus, qui nomen Marcus habebat, dixit, "Lucius, visne ad Senatum mecum venire? Hodie oratores magni de pace et bello loquentur." Lucius laetus consensit et cum Marco ad Senatum perrexit.

Cum ad Senatum pervenissent, Lucius magnas columnas et statuas vidit. Intravit et vidit senatores in togis candidis sedentes, omnes in consilio congregati. Orator stabat et magna voce loquebatur, "Cives Romani, debemusne bellum gerere aut pacem servare?" Lucius, qui solum agriculturam noverat, nunc animadvertebat quantam vim et potestatem Roma haberet. Sensit se parvam partem huius magni mundi esse.

English Translation: After seeing the forum, Lucius heard about the Senate, a great place where Romans made laws. A new friend, named Marcus, said, "Lucius, would you like to come to the Senate with me? Today, great speakers will talk about peace and war." Lucius happily agreed and went to the Senate with Marcus.

When they arrived at the Senate, Lucius saw large columns and statues. He entered and saw senators sitting in their white togas, all gathered in council. An orator stood and spoke in a loud voice, "Roman citizens, should we wage war or preserve peace?" Lucius, who only knew about farming, now realized how much power and authority Rome had. He felt like a small part of this great world.

Page 4: The Gladiator Games

Latin: Postquam Senatum reliquerunt, Marcus Lucium rogavit, "Visne ludos gladiatorum videre? Hodie in Colosseo ludi magnifici erunt." Lucius, quamquam de auditu gladiatorum timidus erat, consensit et cum Marco ad Colosseum iit.

Colosseum erat ingens amphitheatrum, ubi multae turbae congregatae erant. Lucius numquam antea aedificium tam magnum viderat. Cum intravisset, strepitus populi eum circumdedit, et vidit arenam magnam in medio. Gladiatores, armati gladios et scuta, parati erant ad pugnam.

Cum ludi inceperunt, Lucius cum admiratione spectabat. "Hoc est quod Romani vocant ludos?" cogitavit. Vidit gladiatores inter se pugnantes, animalia fera, et aurigas currus agitantibus. Turba clamabat et applaudebat, sed Lucius sensus mixtos habebat—miratio et horror simul.

English Translation: After they left the Senate, Marcus asked Lucius, "Do you want to see the gladiator games? Today there will be magnificent games in the Colosseum." Lucius, although a little scared about hearing of gladiators, agreed and went with Marcus to the Colosseum.

The Colosseum was a huge amphitheater where large crowds were gathered. Lucius had never seen such a large building before. When he entered, the noise of the crowd surrounded him, and he saw the large arena in the middle. The gladiators, armed with swords and shields, were ready to fight.

When the games began, Lucius watched with amazement. "Is this what the Romans call games?" he thought. He saw gladiators fighting each other, wild animals, and charioteers driving their chariots. The crowd shouted and applauded, but Lucius had mixed feelings—admiration and horror at the same time.

Page 5: Reflection and Return Home

Latin: Post ludos gladiatorum, Lucius cum Marco ad forum rediit. "Roma est urbs mirabilis," dixit Lucius, "sed etiam terribilis. Nunc intellego cur pater me huc miserit. Non solum ut frumentum venderem, sed ut de vita Romana discam."

Marcus eum cum laude respondit, "Bene dicis, Luci. Roma est locus magnae gloriae, sed etiam magnae potestatis. Omnia hic vidisti—legem, bellum, pacem, et ludos."

Lucius se paratum sentiebat ad domum redire. Iterum in Siciliam rediit, sed animo mutato. Nunc non solum rusticus erat, sed etiam Romam viderat et multa didicerat. In domum reversus, pater eum interrogavit, "Quid de Roma didicisti, Luci?"

Lucius cum gravitate respondit, "Roma est urbs magnifica et formidabilis, sed nihil est melius quam simplicem vitam in villa rustica agere."

English Translation: After the gladiator games, Lucius returned to the forum with Marcus. "Rome is a marvelous city," said Lucius, "but also a terrifying one. Now I understand why my father sent me here. Not just to sell grain, but to learn about Roman life."

Marcus praised him and replied, "You speak well, Lucius. Rome is a place of great glory, but also of great power. You have seen everything here—the law, war, peace, and games."

Lucius felt ready to return home. He journeyed back to Sicily, but with a changed mind. Now he was not only a country boy, but he had also seen Rome and learned much. When he returned home, his father asked him, "What did you learn about Rome, Lucius?"

Lucius replied seriously, "Rome is a magnificent and formidable city, but nothing is better than living a simple life in the countryside."

Word List:

- **pater** (father) - /pah-tehr/
- **urbs** (city) - /oorbs/
- **senatus** (Senate) - /seh-nah-toos/
- **amicus** (friend) - /ah-mee-koos/
- **ludi** (games) - /loo-dee/
- **gladiator** (gladiator) - /glah-dee-ah-tohr/
- **forum** (forum) - /foh-room/
- **via** (road) - /wee-ah/
- **populus** (people) - /poh-poo-loos/
- **colosseum** (Colosseum) - /koh-los-seh-oom/
- **arena** (arena) - /ah-reh-nah/
- **gladius** (sword) - /glah-dee-oos/
- **scutum** (shield) - /skoo-toom/

- **bellum** (war) - /beh-loom/
- **pax** (peace) - /pahks/
- **domus** (home) - /doh-moos/

Page 6: Drafted into the Army

Latin: Dum Lucius in Sicilia quiete vivit, nuntius ex Roma venit. "Lex nova promulgata est," dixit pater Lucii, "omnes iuvenes validi ad bellum vocantur. Bellum magnum contra Carthaginienses geritur." Lucius, qui nuper Romam visitaverat, nunc militare debebat. Cum timore et spe novorum rerum, se ad militiam paravit.

Cum ad exercitum Romanum pervenisset, Lucius se sub imperio Scipionis Africani invenit, ducis magni et clari. Scipio exercitum ad Africam ducebat ut Carthaginienses vinceret. Lucius, qui antea agricolam fuisse solebat, nunc gladius et scutum in manibus habebat, paratus ad pugnam.

English Translation: While Lucius was living peacefully in Sicily, a messenger came from Rome. "A new law has been proclaimed," said Lucius's father, "all able young men are called to war. A great war is being waged against the Carthaginians." Lucius, who had recently visited Rome, now had to serve in the military. With fear and hope for new experiences, he prepared himself for the army.

When he arrived at the Roman army, Lucius found himself under the command of Scipio Africanus, a great and famous general. Scipio was leading the army to Africa to defeat the Carthaginians. Lucius, who had once been a farmer, now held a sword and shield in his hands, ready for battle.

Page 7: The Voyage to Africa

Latin: Navigatio ad Africam longa et periculosa erat. Lucius numquam antea mare transierat, et nunc navis magna in undis fluctuantibus eum portabat. Milites multi, sicut Lucius, timore et spe mixti erant. Nonnulli de famae et gloriae spe loquebantur, alii de familia et domo relinquenda cogitabant.

Cum tandem Africam attigissent, Lucius terram novam et ignotam vidit. "Hic est locus ubi Carthago sita est," dixit centurio. Lucius in agmine processit, paratus ad pugnam. Scipio, ante milites suos stans, magna voce dixit, "Hodie non solum pro Roma pugnamus, sed etiam pro futuro nostro!"

English Translation: The voyage to Africa was long and dangerous. Lucius had never crossed the sea before, and now a large ship carried him over the rolling waves. Many soldiers, like Lucius, were filled with both fear and hope. Some spoke of hopes for fame and glory, while others thought of the family and home they had left behind.

When they finally reached Africa, Lucius saw a new and unknown land. "This is the place where Carthage is located," said the centurion. Lucius marched forward in the ranks, ready for battle. Scipio, standing before his soldiers, said in a loud voice, "Today we fight not only for Rome, but also for our future!"

Page 8: The Battle of Zama

Latin: In campo apud Zamam, ubi pugna finalis facta est, Lucius magnam multitudinem militum Romanorum et Carthaginiensium vidit. Elephantes Carthaginienses in fronte agminis stabant, bestiae terribiles et magnitudine formidandae. Lucius, quamvis metu perculsus, se paravit ad pugnam.

Cum signum pugnae datum esset, Romani gladiis et pilis Carthaginienses aggressi sunt. Lucius, inter milites pugnans, animadvertit Scipionem in medio proelii stare, ducem fortem et indomitum. "Roma invicta est!" clamavit Scipio, et milites eum secuti sunt.

Lucius gladium suum vibravit et scutum alte tenuit, defensans contra impetum hostium. Pugna aspera erat, sed tandem Carthaginienses, sub Scipionis ductu, superati sunt. Lucius post pugnam lassus sed victor ad castra revertebat.

English Translation: On the field near Zama, where the final battle took place, Lucius saw a great multitude of Roman and Carthaginian soldiers. Carthaginian elephants stood at the front of their line, terrifying beasts of formidable size. Although struck with fear, Lucius prepared himself for battle.

When the signal for battle was given, the Romans attacked the Carthaginians with swords and spears. Lucius, fighting among the soldiers, noticed Scipio standing in the middle of the battle, a strong and relentless leader. "Rome is undefeated!" Scipio shouted, and the soldiers followed him.

Lucius swung his sword and held his shield high, defending against the enemy's onslaught. The battle was fierce, but eventually, the Carthaginians, under Scipio's leadership, were defeated. Lucius, tired but victorious, returned to the camp after the battle.

Page 9: The Return to Rome

Latin: Cum bellum finitum esset, Lucius cum Scipione et exercitu victore ad Romam rediit. Urbs magna laetitia et ovatione eos accepit. Scipio Africanus, nunc heros Romanus, in curru triumphali urbem intravit, cum milites post eum procedentes. Lucius inter milites gloriosus erat, nunc non solum agricola, sed etiam miles Romae.

Cum ad domum in Sicilia rediisset, Lucius patrem suum amplexus est. "Fili mi," inquit pater, "magnum opus fecisti. Nunc vere Romanus es." Lucius cum honore in patria sua vivebat, et saepe filiis suis narrabat de temporibus magnis cum Scipione in Africa.

English Translation: When the war was over, Lucius returned to Rome with Scipio and the victorious army. The city received them with great joy and ovation. Scipio Africanus, now a Roman hero, entered the city in a triumphal chariot, with the soldiers marching behind him. Lucius was among the proud soldiers, now not just a farmer, but also a soldier of Rome.

When he returned home to Sicily, Lucius embraced his father. "My son," his father said, "you have done a great work. Now you are truly a Roman." Lucius lived with honor in his homeland, and often told his children about the great times with Scipio in Africa.

Word List:

- **bellum** (war) - /beh-loom/
- **miles** (soldier) - /mee-les/
- **Roma** (Rome) - /roh-mah/
- **Scipio** (Scipio) - /skee-pee-oh/
- **exercitus** (army) - /ehg-ser-chee-toos/
- **gladius** (sword) - /glah-dee-oos/
- **scutum** (shield) - /skoo-toom/
- **triumphus** (triumph) - /tree-oom-foos/
- **elephantus** (elephant) - /eh-leh-fahn-toos/
- **agricola** (farmer) - /ah-gree-koh-lah/
- **pater** (father) - /pah-tehr/
- **victoria** (victory) - /week-toh-ree-ah/
- **heros** (hero) - /heh-rohs/

Publius Vergilius Maro, known as Virgil, was one of Rome's greatest poets. His epic poem, *Aeneid*, tells the story of Aeneas, a Trojan who traveled to Italy and became the ancestor of the Romans. The *Aeneid* is both a national epic of Rome and a masterpiece of Latin literature. It blends myth, history, and prophecy, celebrating Roman virtues and Augustus' imperial destiny.

Virgil's *Aeneid* (Extended Excerpt with English Translation)

Latin (Lines 1-11):

Arma virumque **cano**, Troiae qui primus ab **oris**
Italiam, fato profugus, Laviniaque **venit**
litora — multum ille et **terris** iactatus et alto
vi superum, saevae memorem Iunonis ob iram,
multa quoque et bello passus, dum conderet urbem,
inferretque deos Latio — genus unde Latinum
Albanique patres, atque altae moenia Romae.

English:

I **sing** of **arms** and the man, who first from the **shores** of Troy,
exiled by fate, came to Italy and the Lavinian **coasts** —
much tossed about both on **land** and on the deep
by the force of the gods, on account of the unforgetting anger of cruel Juno,
also having suffered much in war, until he could found a city
and bring his gods to Latium — from which came the Latin race,
the Alban fathers, and the walls of high Rome.

Latin (Lines 12-18):

Musa, mihi causas memora, quo numine laeso,
quidve dolens, regina deum tot volvere casus
insignem pietate virum, tot adire labores
impulerit. Tantaene animis caelestibus irae?
Urbs antiqua fuit, Tyrii tenuere coloni,
Karthago, Italiam contra Tiberinaque longe
ostia, dives opum studiisque asperrima belli;

English:

Muse, remind me of the reasons, by what divine power having been offended,
or grieving at what, the queen of the gods compelled a man marked by piety
to endure so many misfortunes, to approach so many labors.
Is there so much anger in celestial minds?
There was an ancient city, Tyrian colonists held it,
Carthage, opposite Italy and far from the Tiber's mouths,
rich in resources and very fierce in the pursuits of war;

Latin (Lines 19-26):

quam Iuno fertur terris magis omnibus unam
posthabita coluisse Samo; hic illius arma,
hic currus fuit; hoc regnum dea gentibus esse,
si qua fata sinant, iam tum tenditque fovetque.
Progeniem sed enim Troiano a sanguine duci
audierat, Tyrias olim quae verteret arces;
hinc populum late regem belloque superbum
venturum excidio Libyae: sic volvere Parcas.

English:

which Juno is said to have cherished more than all lands,
even placing Samos after it; here were her **arms**,
here was her chariot; this city, the goddess aimed and cherished
to be the kingdom for the nations, if only the fates would allow.
But indeed, she had heard that a progeny would be led
from Trojan blood, which would one day overturn the Tyrian citadels;
from here would come a people ruling widely and proud in war
for the destruction of Libya: thus the Fates unrolled.

Words Covered in the Book (in Bold):

- **Arma** (arms, weapons) - ar-mah
- **cano** (I sing) - kah-noh
- **oris** (shores, coasts) - oh-rees
- **venit** (he came) - weh-neet
- **litora** (coasts, shores) - lee-toh-rah
- **terris** (lands) - tehr-rees
- **fuit** (was) - foo-it
- **currus** (chariot) - kur-roos

Quintus Horatius Flaccus, known as Horace, was a prominent Roman poet during the reign of Augustus. His *Satires* explore the everyday life and society of Rome with wit and moral insight. Horace uses a conversational tone to critique the vices and absurdities of his contemporaries, often employing humor and irony to make his points. His work remains influential in both literature and moral philosophy.

Horace's *Satires* (Book 1, Satire 1) with English Translation

Latin:

Quid enim? concurritur: **horas** non **num** fit ut **omnes**
cum **duce** formicae **acrobat**, et **ipse volucres**
ipsiusque **capiti**, et mollia cingitur **arma**
mollibus officiis, **locuples** quid? et **cetera** quae vult.

English:

What then? They gather: it often happens that **all** the ants
rush together with their **leader**, and **even** the birds
and their **own** heads are armed with soft **armor**,
wrapped in soft duties, what does the **wealthy** man want? And **the rest** of what he desires.

Latin:

Cur eget indignus **quisquam** te divite? **quare**
templa ruunt antiqua deum? cur, **improbus** iste
sanctus heri **toties** consilio vocatus? at **illud**
utrumque tenerae fugiunt? neque **curat** hic
carnis morbus.

English:

Why does any **undeserving** person want from you, the rich man? **Why**
do the ancient temples of the gods collapse? Why is that **wicked** man
called so often to the council, and yet **yesterday** he fled from both,
and **that** tender **illness** of the flesh did not concern him?

Words Covered in the Book (in Bold)

- **horas** (hours) - hoh-rahss
- **num** (surely, indeed) - noom
- **omnes** (all) - ohm-nehss

- **duce** (leader) - doo-keh
- **ipse** (himself, herself, itself) - ip-seh
- **volucres** (birds) - voh-loo-krehss
- **capiti** (head) - kah-pee-tee
- **arma** (armor, weapons) - ar-mah
- **locuples** (wealthy) - loh-kew-plehs
- **cetera** (the rest, the others) - keh-teh-rah
- **quisquam** (anyone, somebody) - kwees-kwahm
- **quare** (why) - kwah-reh
- **improbus** (wicked) - im-proh-boos
- **toties** (so often) - toh-tee-ehs
- **illud** (that) - il-luhd
- **curat** (he/she/it cares) - koo-raht

Publius Ovidius Naso, commonly known as Ovid, was a Roman poet who lived during the reign of Augustus. His most famous work, *Metamorphoses*, is a narrative poem that compiles over 250 myths, all connected by the theme of transformation. Ovid's poetic style is both sophisticated and vivid, making his tales of gods, heroes, and mythical creatures captivating. *Metamorphoses* has had a lasting influence on Western art and literature, serving as a key source of classical mythology.

Ovid's *Metamorphoses* (Book 1, Lines 89-112) with English Translation

Latin:

Ante **mare** et **terras** et quod tegit **omnia** caelum
unus erat toto naturae vultus in **orbe**,
quem dixere **Chaos**: rudis indigestaque **moles**,
nec quicquam **nisi** pondus **inertiae**, congestaque eodem
non bene iunctarum discordia **semina** rerum.

English:

Before the **sea** and the **lands** and the **sky** that covers **everything**,
there was **one** face of nature in the whole **world**,
which they called **Chaos**: a rough and unformed **mass**,
and nothing **but** the weight of **inactivity**, and the discordant **seeds** of things
piled together in the same place, not well joined.

Latin:

Nullus adhuc **mundo** praebebat **lumina** Titan,
nec nova crescendo reparabat cornua Phoebe,
nec **circumfuso** pendebat in aere tellus
ponderibus librata suis, nec bracchia longo
margine terrarum porrexerat Amphitrite.

English:

As yet no Titan was offering his **light** to the **world**,
nor was Phoebe renewing her horns by growing,
nor was the Earth hanging in the air surrounded
by its own weight, nor had Amphitrite extended
her arms along the long shore of the lands.

Words Covered in the Book (in Bold)

- **mare** (sea) - mah-reh
- **terras** (lands, earth) - tehr-rahs
- **omnia** (everything, all) - ohm-nee-ah
- **unus** (one) - oo-noos
- **orbe** (world, sphere) - or-beh
- **nisi** (but, unless) - nee-see
- **semina** (seeds) - seh-mee-nah
- **mundo** (world) - moon-doh
- **lumina** (lights) - loo-mee-nah
- **circumfuso** (surrounded, poured around) - keer-koom-foo-soh

Marcus Aurelius (121-180 AD) was a Roman emperor and Stoic philosopher, best known for his work *Meditations*, a series of personal writings that reflect his Stoic beliefs. As one of the last five *Good Emperors* of Rome, Marcus Aurelius ruled with a sense of duty and moral integrity. *Meditations* was written during his military campaigns, where he often reflected on life, virtue, and human nature. The work is a guide to personal ethics, emphasizing self-discipline, the transience of life, and the importance of reason over emotion.

Below is an excerpt from *Meditations* in Latin, with translations and key Latin vocabulary highlighted in bold for students of Latin.

Marcus Aurelius' *Meditations* (Excerpt)

Latin:

Saepe cogita quam multa tibi fugienda sint, et quid sit quod bonam vitam efficiat. **Non** res externas specta, sed **in** te ipsum reverti. Ne **mores** hominum corrumpant tuam **mentem**. Si quid mali in **vita** tua fuerit, tuum est emendare; si quid boni, conservare. **Vita** quidem brevis est, sed recte vivendi occasio aeterna. Omnia quae vides, fluxa sunt, ut **tempus** quod fugit. Nihil **permanet**, omnia mutantur.

English:

Consider often how many things you must avoid, and what it is that makes a good life. **Do not** look at external things, but rather turn back **within** yourself. Let not the **ways** of men corrupt your **mind**. If there is any evil in your **life**, it is yours to correct; if there is any good, it is yours to preserve. **Life** is indeed short, but the opportunity to live rightly is eternal. All that you see is fleeting, like the **time** that passes. Nothing **remains**; everything changes.

Latin:

Memento te hominem esse: fragilis corporis et mortalem, sed **mentis** potens et rationis amantem. **Non** tibi longum tempus in **vita** restat, sed quod restat, bene vive et **virtutem** cole. **Mors** non terribilis est, nisi **mentem** turbat. Qui ad **naturam** vivit, **mori** non timet, quoniam nihil est in morte quod **vitam** corrumpat.

English:

Remember that you are human: of a fragile body and mortal, but powerful in **mind** and a lover of reason. **Do not** think that you have much time left in **life**, but what remains, live well and cultivate **virtue**. **Death** is not terrifying unless it disturbs the **mind**. He who lives according to **nature** does not fear **death**, for there is nothing in death that corrupts **life**.

Latin:

Vive cum **virtute** et honore. **Vita** brevis est, sed tantum valet quantum **virtus** eam facit. Ne mortem **time**, sed virtutem **ama**. **Non** timenda est **mors**, quia est **naturae** pars. Omnia quae sunt et erunt, secundum **naturam** eveniunt.

English:

Live with **virtue** and honor. **Life** is short, but it is worth as much as **virtue** makes it. Fear not death, but love **virtue**. **Do not** fear **death**, for it is part of **nature**. All things that are and will be come about according to **nature**.

Latin:

Omnia fluxa sunt et caduca. **Tempus** quod fugit, et **vita** quae labitur, nos admonent ne rebus externis nimium tribuamus. **Non** est **mors** quae metum parit, sed metus **mortis**. Qui mortem accipit cum quiete animi, **vir** sapiens est. Ne discas **mortem** metuere, sed discas cum **vita** recte agere.

English:

All things are fleeting and perishable. **Time** that passes and **life** that slips away remind us not to give too much importance to external things. It is **not death** that causes fear, but the fear of **death**. He who accepts death with a calm mind is a wise **man**. Learn not to fear **death**, but rather learn to live **life** rightly.

Latin:

Nihil est quod **mortem** metuas, cum **vita** ipsa brevis sit et transitoria. Memento vivere cum **virtute**, nec ullum tempus **tempus** terere. **Vita** est brevis, sed longior fit recte vivendo. Omnia quae secundum **naturam** sunt, bona sunt.

English:

There is no reason to fear **death**, for **life** itself is short and fleeting. Remember to live with **virtue**, and waste no **time**. **Life** is short, but it becomes longer by living rightly. All things according to **nature** are good.

Word List

1. **Non** - not / no (Latin: nohn)
2. **In** - in / on (Latin: ihn)

3. **Mores** - ways / customs (Latin: moh-res)
4. **Mentem** - mind (Latin: men-tem)
5. **Vita** - life (Latin: vee-tah)
6. **Tempus** - time (Latin: tem-poos)
7. **Permanet** - remains / endures (Latin: per-mah-net)
8. **Memento** - remember (Latin: meh-men-toh)
9. **Virtutem** - virtue (Latin: weer-too-tem)
10. **Mors** - death (Latin: mohrs)
11. **Naturae** - nature (Latin: nah-too-rye)
12. **Mori** - to die (Latin: moh-ree)
13. **Ama** - love (Latin: ah-mah)
14. **Vir** - man (Latin: weer)

Lucius Annaeus Seneca (c. 4 BC – AD 65), commonly known as Seneca the Younger, was a Roman Stoic philosopher, statesman, and playwright. He is best known for his philosophical essays and letters that explore Stoic philosophy, as well as his tragedies. Seneca served as an advisor to Emperor Nero, and his writings reflect his thoughts on ethics, the nature of the soul, and how to live a good life according to Stoic principles. His works are still widely read today for their profound insights into human nature and the art of living.

Below is an excerpt from Seneca's writings, with translations provided for each section. Key Latin vocabulary words that have been covered so far in this book are highlighted in bold.

Seneca's *Letters to Lucilius* (Excerpt)

Latin:

Vita si scias uti, longa est. Sed plerique **non** vitam, sed **tempus** perditum **esse** queruntur. Non accipimus brevem vitam, sed fecimus; **non** inopes eius, sed prodigi sumus.

English:

Life is long if you know how to use it. But most people complain that **life** is short, not because **it** is, but because they waste **time**. We are not given a short life, but we make **it** so; we are not short of **time**, but wasteful.

Latin:

Tempus nec avocatur nec **revocatur**; quidquid **tempus** recipis, nec **redditur** nec **revertitur**. Non est **vita** brevis, sed brevi **vita** abutimur. **Vita** satis longa est, et in maximis rebus sufficienter data est.

English:

Time is neither called back nor **recalled**; whatever **time** you receive is neither **given back** nor **returned**. **Life** is not short, but we make **it** short. **Life** is long enough, and **it** is sufficiently given for the greatest things.

Latin:

Quid de **morte** timemus? Si **vita** recte agitur, **mors** non terribilis est. Non est, quod **mortem** metuas; **mors** enim nihil est nisi ultimus **vitae** actus.

English:

Why do we fear **death**? If **life** is lived rightly, **death** is not terrifying. There is no reason to fear **death**; **death** is nothing but the final act of **life**.

Latin:

Quid prodest homini **tempus** servare et vitam perdere? **Tempus** fugit, et cum illo **vita**. Ergo, **vita** sicut aurum custodienda est.

English:

What does it profit a man to save **time** and lose **life**? **Time** flies, and with it **life**. Therefore, **life** must be guarded like gold.

Latin:

Non licet tibi **vitam** iterum inchoare; nam **vita** quidem cursus est, non cursus interruptus. Omne **tempus** praeteritum nec **revertitur** nec **revocatur**; **vita** fluit, et **tempus** cum illa.

English:

You are not allowed to start **life** over again; for **life** is indeed a course, not an interrupted course. All **time** past neither **returns** nor **is recalled**; **life** flows, and **time** with it.

Latin:

Facile est **vitam** perdere in vanis studiis, et **vita** consumitur **non** in rebus necessariis, sed in superfluis. **Vita** fugax est, et qui **tempus** contemnit, **vitam** contemnit.

English:

It is easy to waste **life** in vain pursuits, and **life** is consumed **not** by necessary things, but by the superfluous. **Life** is fleeting, and he who despises **time**, despises **life**.

Word List

1. **Vita** - life (Latin: vee-tah)
2. **Non** - not / no (Latin: nohn)
3. **Tempus** - time (Latin: tem-poos)
4. **Esse** - to be (Latin: es-seh)
5. **Revocatur** - recalled (Latin: reh-voh-kah-toor)
6. **Reddere** - to give back (Latin: red-deh-reh)
7. **Revertitur** - returns (Latin: reh-ver-ti-toor)
8. **Mors** - death (Latin: mohrs)
9. **Mortem** - death (accusative form) (Latin: mohr-tem)
10. **Vitae** - of life (Latin: vee-tye)
11. **Inchoare** - to start (Latin: in-koh-ah-reh)

Marcus Tullius Cicero (106 BC – 43 BC) was one of Rome's greatest orators, statesmen, and philosophers. His influence on the Latin language was so profound that subsequent generations of Latin speakers and writers considered his style as the pinnacle of Latin prose. Cicero's writings covered a wide range of topics, including politics, philosophy, and rhetoric. His works remain essential reading for those interested in Roman history, rhetoric, and the development of Western philosophy.

Below is an excerpt from Cicero's works, followed by a translation. Key Latin vocabulary words that have been covered in this book are highlighted in bold.

Cicero's *De Amicitia* (On Friendship) (Excerpt)

Latin:

Amicitia enim **non** solum **ipsa** sibi **honesta** est, sed etiam **omnium** aliarum **rerum honestas** oritur **ex ea**.

English:

Friendship is not only **honorable** in **itself**, but the **honor** of all other **things** arises **from it**.

Latin:

Nam **virtus amicitiam** gignit, nec sine **virtute amicitia** esse ullo pacto potest.

English:

For **virtue** gives birth to **friendship**, and without **virtue friendship** cannot exist in any way.

Latin:

Verum hoc se habet, quod **amicitia non** satis **natura** ac **mores** humani sunt: **amicitiam** non posse nisi **inter bonos** esse.

English:

But this is true, that **friendship** is not sufficiently within **human nature** and **morals**: **friendship** cannot exist except **among** the **good**.

Latin:

Sed si forte **amicitia** illa vera et perfecta sit, tamen, **quoniam** rara est, **amicitia** ipsa delectat, etiam si minime **necessaria** est.

English:

But if by chance that **friendship** is true and perfect, nevertheless, since it is rare, **friendship** itself is delightful, even if it is not **necessary** at all.

Latin:

Non est autem vera **amicitia** nisi **inter bonos**; neque enim **malus amicum** habere potest.

English:

However, **true friendship** does not exist except **among** the **good**; for the **wicked** cannot have a **friend**.

Latin:

Amicitia vero **posita** est in **probitate** et **virtute**, **honestas** enim **coniungit** eos qui **amicitiam** fovent, et sine **honestate** non potest esse **amicitia**.

English:

Friendship is truly based on **honesty** and **virtue**, for **honor** unites those who nurture **friendship**, and without **honesty**, **friendship** cannot exist.

Word List

1. **Amicitia** - friendship (Latin: ah-mee-kee-tee-ah)
2. **Non** - not / no (Latin: nohn)
3. **Ipsa** - itself (Latin: eep-sah)
4. **Honesta** - honorable (Latin: hoh-neh-stah)
5. **Omnium** - of all (Latin: ohm-nee-oom)
6. **Rerum** - of things (Latin: reh-room)
7. **Ex** - from / out of (Latin: eks)
8. **Ea** - it / she (Latin: eh-ah)
9. **Virtus** - virtue (Latin: weer-toos)
10. **Inter** - among / between (Latin: in-ter)
11. **Bonos** - the good (Latin: boh-nohs)
12. **Quoniam** - since (Latin: kwoh-nee-am)
13. **Necessaria** - necessary (Latin: neh-keh-sah-ree-ah)
14. **Malus** - wicked / evil (Latin: mah-loos)
15. **Posita** - placed / based (Latin: poh-see-tah)
16. **Probitate** - honesty / probity (Latin: proh-bee-tah-teh)
17. **Coniungit** - unites / joins together (Latin: koh-nyoon-geet)

Gaius Julius Caesar (100 BC – 44 BC) was a Roman general, statesman, and author who played a critical role in the events that led to the downfall of the Roman Republic and the rise of the Roman Empire. He is widely remembered not only for his military conquests but also for his writings, particularly *Commentarii de Bello Gallico* (The Gallic Wars), where he detailed his campaigns in Gaul. This work is a significant piece of Latin literature and provides insight into Caesar's military strategies and the broader context of Roman history during his time.

Below is an excerpt from Julius Caesar's *Commentarii de Bello Gallico*, followed by an English translation. Key Latin vocabulary words that have been covered in this book are highlighted in **bold**.

Julius Caesar's *Commentarii de Bello Gallico* (The Gallic Wars) (Excerpt)

Latin:

Gallia est omnis divisa in partes tres, quarum unam incolunt **Belgae**, aliam **Aquitani**, tertiam qui ipsorum **lingua Celtae, nostra Galli** appellantur. Hi omnes **lingua, institutis**, legibus inter se differunt. **Gallos** ab **Aquitaniis Garumna** flumen, a **Belgis Matrona** et **Sequana** dividit.

English:

Gaul as a whole is divided into three parts, one of which the **Belgae** inhabit, another the **Aquitani**, and the third by those who in their own **language** are called **Celts**, in **our Gauls**. All these differ from one another in **language**, customs, and laws. The **Garumna** river divides the **Gauls** from the **Aquitani**, and the **Matrona** and **Sequana** rivers divide them from the **Belgae**.

Latin:

Horum omnium **fortissimi** sunt **Belgae**, propterea quod a cultu atque humanitate provinciae longissime absunt, minimeque ad eos mercatores saepe commeant atque ea quae ad effeminandos animos pertinent important, proximique sunt **Germanis**, qui trans **Rhenum** incolunt, quibuscum continenter bellum gerunt. Qua de causa **Helvetii** quoque reliquos **Gallos** virtute praecedunt, quod fere cotidianis proeliis cum **Germanis** contendunt, cum aut suis finibus eos prohibent aut ipsi in eorum finibus bellum gerunt.

English:

Of all these, the **Belgae** are the **bravest**, because they are the farthest removed from the culture and civilization of the province, and merchants least frequently resort to them, bringing in those things that tend to weaken the spirit, and they are nearest to the **Germans**, who dwell beyond the **Rhine**, with whom they are continually waging war. For this reason, the **Helvetii** also surpass the rest of the **Gauls** in courage, because they fight with the **Germans** in almost daily battles, either repelling them from their own borders or themselves waging war in the territory of the **Germans**.

Latin:

Apud **Helvetios** longe nobilissimus fuit et ditissimus **Orgetorix**. Is **M. Messala**, et **M. Pisone** consulibus, regni cupiditate inductus coniurationem nobilitatis fecit et civitati persuasit ut de finibus suis cum omnibus copiis exirent: perfacile esse, cum virtute omnibus praestarent, totius **Galliae** imperio potiri. Id hoc facilius iis persuasit, quod undique loci natura **Helvetii** continentur: una ex parte **flumine Rheno** latissimo atque altissimo, qui agrum **Helvetium** a **Germanis** dividit; altera ex parte **monte Iura** altissimo, qui est inter **Sequanos** et **Helvetios**; tertia lacu **Lemanno** et **flumine Rhodano**, qui provinciam nostram ab **Helvetiis** dividit.

English:

Among the **Helvetii** the most distinguished and wealthiest by far was **Orgetorix**. During the consulship of **Marcus Messala** and **Marcus Piso**, he, driven by a desire for kingship, formed a conspiracy among the nobility and persuaded his fellow citizens to leave their borders with all their forces; asserting that it would be very easy to acquire control of all **Gaul**, since they surpassed everyone in courage. He persuaded them more easily to do this because the **Helvetii** are confined by the nature of their location: on one side by the **Rhine**, a river of great width and depth, which separates the **Helvetian** territory from the **Germans**; on another side by the very high **Jura** mountains, which lie between the **Sequani** and the **Helvetii**; on the third side by **Lake Geneva** and by the **Rhone**, a river that separates our province from the **Helvetii**.

Latin:

His rebus adducti et auctoritate **Orgetorigis** permoti constituerunt ea quae ad proficiscendum pertinerent comparare, iumentorum et carrorum quam maximum numerum coemere, sementes quam maximas facere, ut in itinere copia frumenti suppeteret, cum proximis civitatibus pacem et amicitiam confirmare. Ad eas res conficiendas **biennium** sibi satis esse duxerunt; in tertium annum profectionem lege confirmant. Ad eas res conficiendas **Orgetorix** deligitur. Is sibi **legationem** ad civitates suscipit.

English:

Influenced by these factors and moved by **Orgetorix's** authority, they decided to prepare the things needed for their departure: to buy up as many beasts of burden and carts as possible, to make their sowings as extensive as possible, so that during their journey an ample supply of grain would be available, and to establish peace and friendship with the neighboring states. They considered two years sufficient to complete these preparations; they establish by law their departure for the third year. **Orgetorix** was chosen to complete these preparations. He undertook the task of sending envoys to the states.

Word List

- **Gallia** - Gaul (GAHL-lee-ah)
- **Belgae** - Belgians (BELL-gai)
- **Aquitani** - Aquitanians (ah-kee-TAH-nee)
- **lingua** - language (LING-gwah)
- **Celtae** - Celts (KELL-tai)
- **nostra** - our (NOS-trah)
- **Galli** - Gauls (GAHL-lee)
- **fortissimi** - bravest (for-TEESS-si-mee)
- **Germanis** - Germans (ger-MAHN-is)
- **Helvetii** - Helvetians (hel-VEH-tee-eye)
- **Rhenum** - Rhine (RAY-num)
- **flumine** - river (FLOO-mee-neh)
- **Sequana** - Seine (SEH-kwah-nah)
- **femina** - woman (FEH-mee-nah)
- **imperio** - command, rule (im-PAY-ree-oh)
- **mons** - mountain (mons)
- **copia** - supply, abundance (KOH-pee-ah)
- **legatio** - embassy, mission (leh-GAH-tee-oh)
- **biennium** - two years (bee-EN-nee-um)

Pliny the Elder, born Gaius Plinius Secundus in AD 23, was a Roman author, naturalist, and philosopher, most famous for his work "Naturalis Historia" (Natural History), an extensive encyclopedia that covers various topics such as geography, anthropology, biology, and mineralogy. His works provide invaluable insights into the Roman world and its understanding of nature and the wider world. Pliny's detailed accounts often reflect the knowledge and myths of his time, making his writings a crucial resource for understanding ancient Roman thought and culture.

Pliny the Elder's Naturalis Historia with English Translation

Latin:

simili modo et de **mensura** eius varia prodidere, primus dalion ultra **meroën** longe subvectus, mox aristocreon et bion et basilis, simonides minor etiam quinquennio in **meroë** moratus, cum de **aethiopia** scriberet. nam timosthenes, classium philadelphi praefectus, sine **mensura** dierum lx a **syene meroën** iter prodidit, eratosthenes, artemidorus, sebosus ab **aegypti** extremis, unde proxime dicti.

English:

In a similar manner, various authors have reported different accounts of its **measurement**: first, Dalion, who sailed far beyond **Meroe**; then Aristocreon, Bion, and Basilis; and Simonides the Younger, who stayed in **Meroe** for five years when he wrote about **Ethiopia**. For Timosthenes, the commander of the fleets of Philadelphus, gave an account of the journey from **Syene** to **Meroe** without specifying the number of days, while Eratosthenes, Artemidorus, and Sebosus reported different distances from the farthest parts of **Egypt**.

Latin:

verum omnis haec finita nuper disputatio est, quoniam a **syene** neronis exploratores renuntiavere his modis: a **syene hieran sycaminon** p., inde **tama** regione euonymiton **aethiopum**, primi, **acinam**, **pitaram**, **tergedum**. insulam **gagauden** esse in medio eo tractu; inde primum visas aves psittacos et ab altera, quae vocetur **artigula**, animal sphingion, a **tergedo** cynocephalos.

English:

However, all this discussion was recently settled, as Nero's explorers reported the following distances from **Syene**: from **Syene** to **Hieran Sycamion** 54 miles, then to **Tama** in the region of the left side of the **Ethiopians**, to **Acinam**, to **Pitara**, to **Tergedum**. **Gagauden Island** lies in the middle of this region; from there, parrots were first seen, and from another place called **Artigula**, the sphinx-like animal, and from **Tergedum**, the dog-headed baboons.

Latin:

inde **nabata**; oppidum id parvum inter praedicta solum. ab eo ad insulam **meroën**. herbas circa **meroën** demum viridiores, silvarumque aliquid apparuisse et rhinocerotum elephantorumque vestigia. ipsum oppidum **meroën** ab introitu insulae abesse, iuxtaque aliam insulam **tadu** dextro subeuntibus alveo, quae portum faceret.

English:

From there, **Nabata**; a small town among those mentioned earlier. From it to the island of **Meroe**. Near **Meroe** the grass becomes greener, and traces of rhinos and elephants appear. The town of **Meroe** is located 70 miles from the entrance of the island, and next to it is another island, **Tadu**, on the right side of the channel, forming a port.

Latin:

aedificia oppidi pauca; regnare feminam candacen, quod nomen multis iam annis ad reginas transiit; delubrum hammonis et ibi religiosum et toto tractu sacella. cetero cum potirentur rerum **aethiopes**, insula ea magnae claritatis fuit. tradunt armatorum dare solitam, artificum. alii reges **aethiopum** esse hodie traduntur. universa vero gens aetheria appellata est, deinde atlantia, mox a vulcani filio aethiope. animalium hominumque monstrificas effigies circa extremitates eius gigni minime mirum, artifici ad formanda corpora effigiesque caelandas mobilitate ignea. ferunt certe ab orientis parte intima gentes esse sine naribus, aequali totius oris planitie, alias superiore labro orbas, alias sine linguis. pars etiam ore concreto et naribus carens uno tantum foramine spirat potumque calamis avenae trahit et grana eiusdem avenae sponte provenientis ad vescendum. quibusdam pro sermone nutus motusque membrorum est. quibusdam ante **ptolemaeum lathyrum** regem **aegypti** ignotus fuit usus ignium. quidam et pygmaeorum gentem prodiderunt inter paludes ex quibus **nilus** oriretur. in ora autem ubi dicemus continui montes ardentibus similes rubent.

English:

The buildings of the town are few; a woman named Candace rules, a name that has passed to the queens for many years; there is a temple of Ammon, and in that place, it is sacred, with shrines throughout the region. While the **Ethiopians** held power, this island was of great fame. They say it could provide 250 armed men and 3,000 artisans. Some say there are still 45 kings of the **Ethiopians** today. The entire nation was once called Aetheria, then Atlantia, later named after the son of Vulcan, Aethiops. It is not surprising that monstrous shapes of animals and humans are born around its extremities, shaped by the fiery energy that creates their forms. They say that from the deepest parts of the east, there are people without noses, with a flat surface across their entire face, others without upper lips, and some without tongues. Some even breathe through a single hole and drink through a straw, consuming the grains of wild oats that grow there spontaneously. For some, gestures and movements of the limbs serve as their speech. For some, the use of fire was unknown before the reign of **Ptolemy Lathyrus**, king of **Egypt**. Some also reported a nation of **Pygmies** among the swamps where the **Nile** rises. On the coast, where we shall speak of it, continuous mountains glow red as if on fire.

Words Covered (in Bold)

- **mensura** (measurement) - meh-soo-rah
- **Meroe** (a place in ancient Ethiopia) - meh-roh-eh
- **Aethiopia** (Ethiopia) - ee-thee-oh-pee-ah
- **Syene** (an ancient city in Egypt) - see-eh-neh
- **Aegypti** (of Egypt) - eh-gip-tee
- **aetheria** (aerial, ethereal) - eh-theh-ree-ah
- **insula** (island) - een-soo-lah
- **aedificia** (buildings) - eh-dee-fee-see-ah
- **regnare** (to rule) - reg-nah-reh
- **artificum** (craftsmen) - ar-tee-fee-koom

When beginning your journey into the Latin language, it's important to start with texts that are approachable and gradually work your way toward more complex literature. Here's a recommended progression of Latin texts, starting from the simplest and advancing to more challenging works as your proficiency grows.

For beginners, **"Puer Romanus"** and **"Colloquia Personarum"** by C. H. Hermansen are excellent starting points. These texts, written in simple Latin, introduce learners to the language through basic stories and dialogues set in ancient Rome. The vocabulary is straightforward, and the grammar is not overly complex, making them accessible to those who are just beginning to learn Latin.

As you gain confidence, you can move on to **"Fabulae Faciles"** by Francis Ritchie. This collection of myths and stories, including famous tales such as the adventures of Hercules and Perseus, is written in Latin that is still simple but slightly more advanced than that found in "Puer Romanus." These stories not only help reinforce your Latin but also introduce you to classical mythology.

Once you are comfortable with intermediate-level Latin, it's time to dive into some of the most famous works of Roman literature. **Ovid's "Metamorphoses"** is a fantastic choice for those ready to explore more complex syntax and poetic language. The "Metamorphoses" is a narrative poem that tells various myths and legends, rich with imagery and literary devices, offering both a challenge and an insight into Roman culture and literature.

Another important text for intermediate students is **"Caesar's Commentarii de Bello Gallico"** (Commentaries on the Gallic War). This work is written in prose and is relatively straightforward in terms of vocabulary and grammar, making it an ideal next step for learners. Caesar's clear and concise style is excellent for those transitioning from beginner texts to more sophisticated Latin literature.

For those advancing further, **Virgil's "Aeneid"** is an essential read. This epic poem is not only a cornerstone of Latin literature but also offers complex sentence structures, a vast array of vocabulary, and deep thematic content. The "Aeneid" requires a solid understanding of Latin but rewards the reader with its rich storytelling and poetic brilliance.

Finally, as you approach an advanced level, you can tackle **Cicero's orations**, such as **"Pro Archia Poeta"** or **"In Catilinam"**. Cicero's Latin is known for its complexity and rhetorical flourish, making his works challenging but deeply rewarding. Reading Cicero allows you to explore the art of Roman oratory and gain insight into the political and cultural life of Rome.

By following this progression—from simple dialogues to the masterpieces of Latin literature—you can gradually build your Latin skills and appreciation for the language. Each text offers unique challenges and rewards, helping you to master the intricacies of Latin while immersing yourself in the rich literary tradition of ancient Rome.

FINAL NOTES

As we turn the final page of this guide, it's important to remember that unlike a work of fiction, which may sit untouched on a shelf after the first read, this book demands your ongoing attention. It is designed to be your constant companion on the journey to language proficiency. Revisit it frequently, dedicating time to practice, memorize words and phrases, and deepen your understanding of grammatical concepts. Aim for a level of familiarity where the language feels intuitive, where words and their meanings come to you effortlessly without the need to consult a dictionary. Achieving this fluency is undoubtedly challenging and requires more than passive study; it necessitates active engagement and immersion in the language on a daily basis if possible!

Remember, language proficiency can diminish over time if not regularly used—a phenomenon often summarized by the saying, "Use it or lose it." It's natural to feel disheartened if, after a period of time, the language seems to have faded from your memory. However, this can be mitigated by integrating Latin into your daily life through reading and other repetition such as watching movies that are fully in Latin. Several movies feature significant Latin dialogue, including **The Passion of the Christ** (2004), which depicts the final hours of Jesus's life, **Sebastiane** (1976), a film about Saint Sebastian entirely in Latin, **La vita nuova** (2008), an experimental adaptation of Dante's work, **The Mill and the Cross** (2011), which includes Latin in a historical exploration of Bruegel's painting, and the planned film **A Canticle for Leibowitz**, based on the novel that heavily features Latin in its post-apocalyptic narrative.

This book was born out of a personal journey navigating the complexities of learning Latin. My aim was to create an accessible, comprehensive language guide that fills in the gaps left by traditional textbooks and many of the other books I have read, all while keeping it affordable for everyone interested in mastering the language. This project is a labor of love and operates on a non-profit basis.

Your insights and experiences are invaluable to me. If you have suggestions for enhancing future editions or if you notice any errors that may have slipped through due to the extensive scope of content, I warmly welcome your feedback. Please feel free to reach out with your thoughts at info@vidart.org.

In closing, mastering Latin is no small feat, but with patience, the right strategies, and the resources provided in this book, progress is within your reach. I hope this guide serves as a valuable tool in your language learning odyssey. Here's to your success—may your journey be eye-opening and enjoyable. *Bona fortuna et gaude in via tua!*

About the Author

Michael Szymczyk is an independent filmmaker, photographer, philosopher and novelist. He is the writer and director of six feature films: *Scent, Eaters of the Dead, SARS-29, Journey to the End of the Night, Night of the Skinwalkers* and *The Reality of Time*. He is also the author of *Atlantis & Its Fate In The Postdiluvian World: A Possible Site for Plato's Atlantis by Kodiak Island, Independent Filmmaking 101, Cinematography 101, Toilet, Tristan MacArthur in the 36th Century, Ancient Philosophy 101, Hyperborea & The Lost Age of Man, A Beginner's Guide to 19th Century German Philosophy, German 101 and several other language learning books.*